EMBROIDERY

Jane Simpson

Contents

This edition first published 1977 by
Octopus Books Limited
59 Grosvenor Street, London W1

Copyright © 1977 Octopus Books Ltd

ISBN 0 7064 0639 7

Produced and printed in Hong Kong by
Mandarin Publishers Limited
22A Westlands Road, Quarry Bay

Frontispiece: Embroidered patchwork pram cover

Photographs on pages 21, 23, 62 by courtesy of
the Victoria and Albert Museum, London
All other photography by Jason Biggs Studio

Introduction

There are so many different types of embroidery that it is impossible to include them all in this book. I have tried to give interesting uses to several types of embroidery and hope that you will be inspired to find out more about this rapidly expanding craft.

Embroidery terminology and the equipment and materials available vary from country to country. Square brackets, [ ], throughout the text denotes equivalent term or material where this differs from the standard British expression.

Apart from the equivalent threads quoted in the text, Coats and Clark stranded embroidery cotton may be substituted for other stranded cottons.

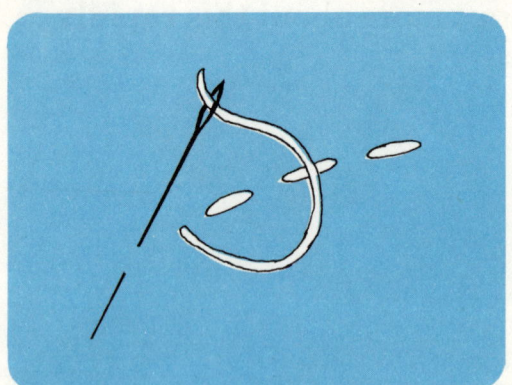

Running stitch

This stitch is worked by passing the needle under and over the fabric. The underneath stitches should all be the same size as each other and half the size of the upper stitches.

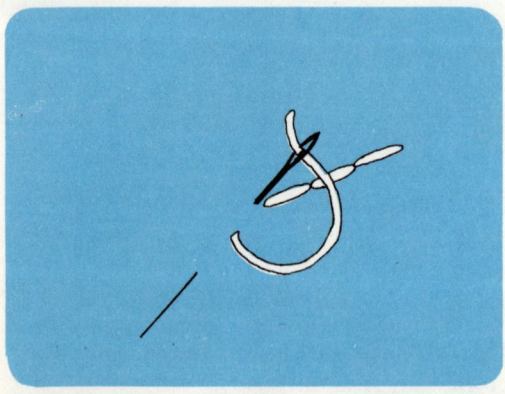

Backstitch

Bring the needle through the fabric and make a small backward stitch. Bring the needle through the fabric again, the same distance in front of the first stitch as the first stitch is long. Insert the needle at the point where it first came through.

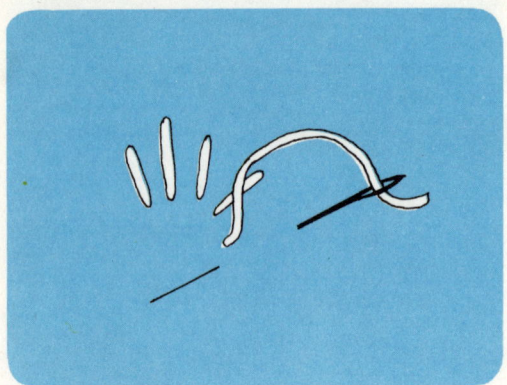

Straight stitch

This is a single stitch which can be regular or irregular and can vary in length.

Illustration opposite shows owl cushion cover, machine embroidered wastepaper bin, nursery panel, embroidered felt ball

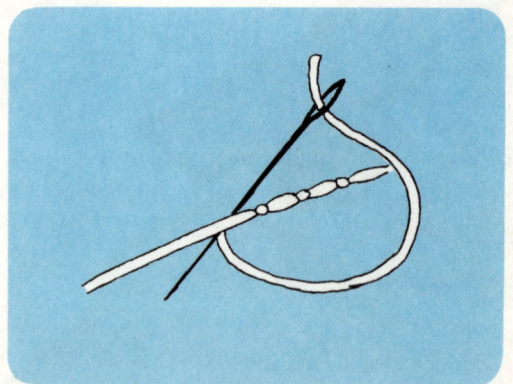

Couching

Lay the thread to be couched on the fabric and sew it in place with small stitches in the same or a contrasting colour thread.

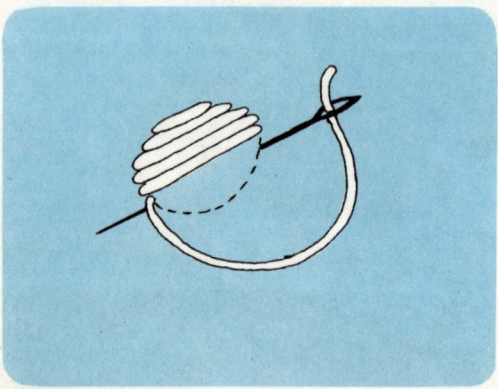

Satin stitch

This stitch consists of straight stitches worked side by side. It is usually used to fill in small shapes and the length can be varied to suit the outline.

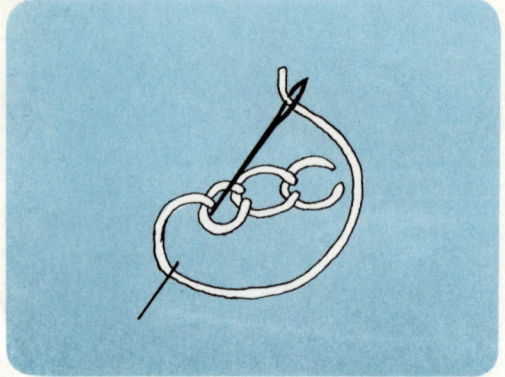

Chain stitch

Bring the needle up through the fabric and, making a loop with the thread, insert it in the same place. Bring the needle up again, through the loop, a short distance in front of where the needle was first brought through.

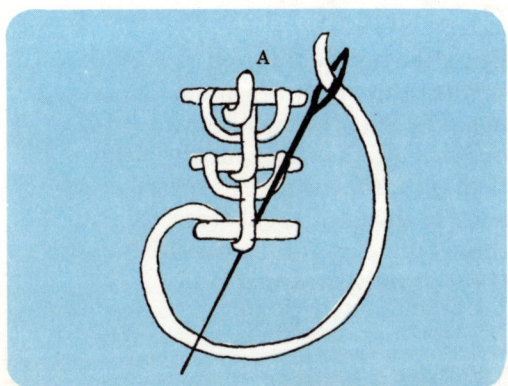

Raised chain band

Work a row of straight stitches fairly close together, as a foundation [initial] row. Bring the needle through at A and push it upwards, under the first bar, to the left of A. Keeping the thread under the needle, push the needle downwards to the right of A, making a chain loop. Carry on, making sure not to pierce the material at all.

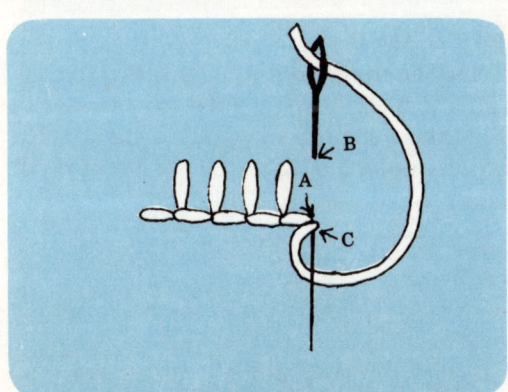

Buttonhole stitch

Work from the left to the right. Bring the thread through at A, insert again at B and bring out through the loop made, at C.

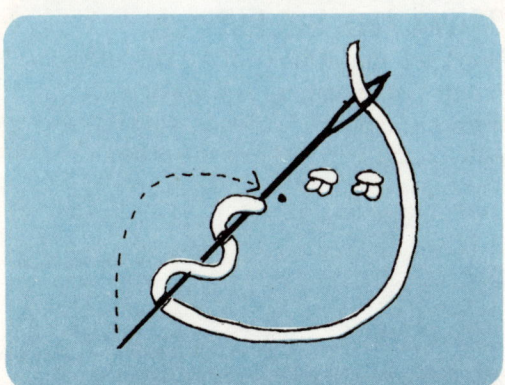

French knot

Bring the needle through the fabric, wrap the thread round the needle (the number of times depends on the size of the knot) and insert the needle again, close to where it came up.

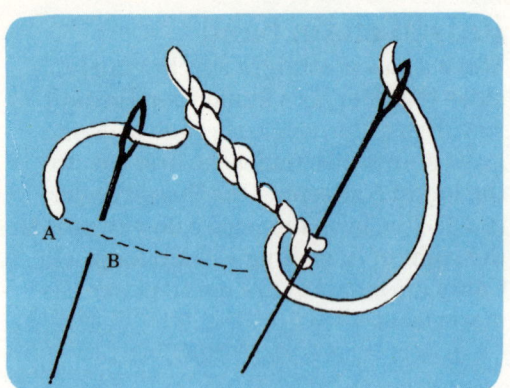

Knot stitch

Bring the needle through at A. Make a small stitch under the guide line, emerging at B. Pass the needle downwards underneath the stitch on the surface, then repeat the same downward movement of the needle, but this time with the thread underneath the needle. Pull the thread firmly to form a knot.

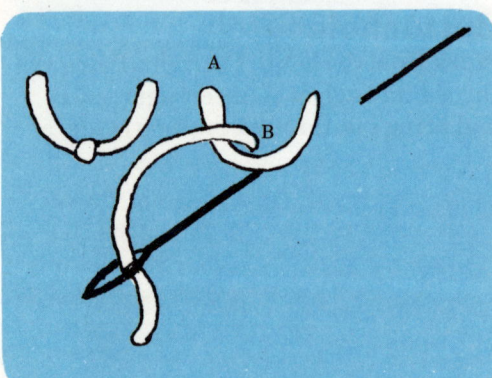

Fly stitch

Bring the needle out at A. Insert it to the right of A and bring it through again at B. Make a small backstitch to anchor the stitch in place. This stitch can be worked singly or in a vertical line.

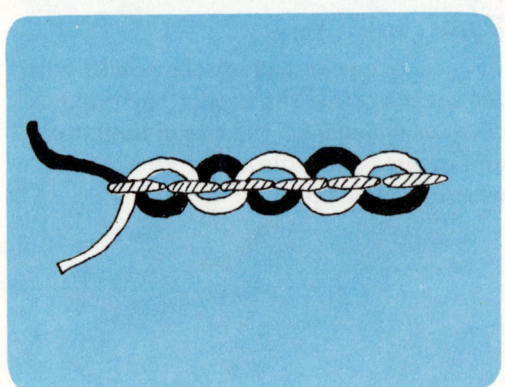

Threaded backstitch

Work a foundation [initial] row of backstitch and thread up and down with different coloured threads working one colour one way and one the other.

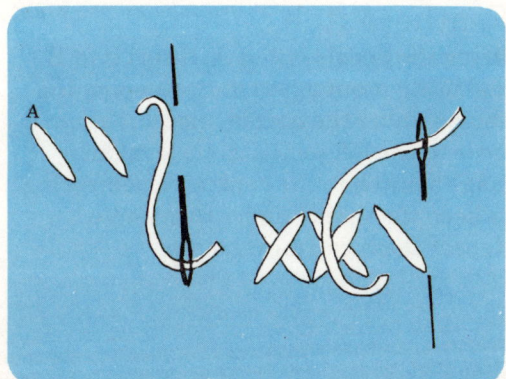

Cross stitch

This stitch is worked from left to right on a fabric with an even weave or a checked pattern. Bring the needle through at A and work a row of sloping stitches all over the same number of threads. Return to the starting point and make another row of stitches over the top of the first row, as shown in the diagram.

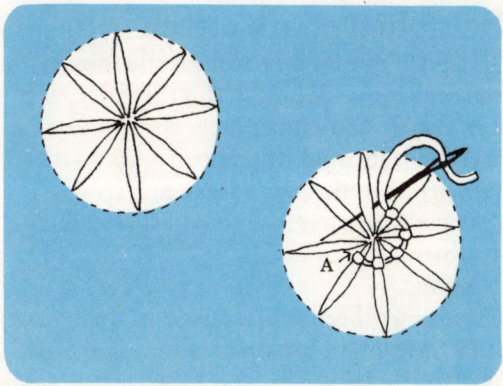

Backstitch spider's web

Using a circle as a guide, work eight evenly spaced stitches into the centre of the circle. Bring the needle out at A and, working anti-clockwise, take the needle under the first straight stitch, without piercing the material. Then thread the needle under the same stitch in the same direction as you did first working a backstitch. Carry on around the circle filling it in.

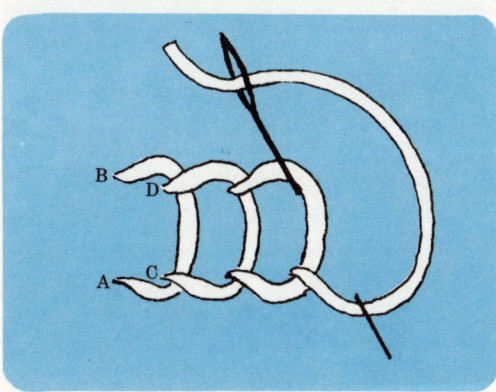

Open chain stitch

This stitch can be used for shapes that vary in width. Bring the needle through at A and, holding the thread with your left thumb, insert it again at B. Bring it through again at C and insert it again at D with the thread under the needle.

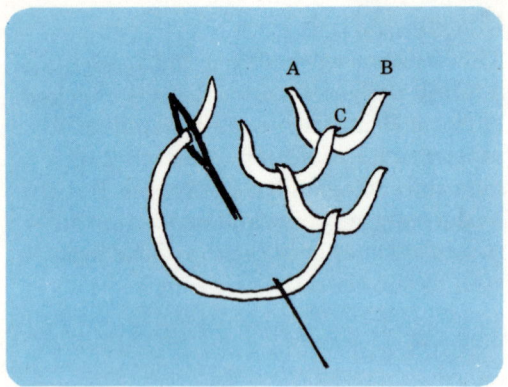

Featherstitch

Bring the needle out at A, insert it at B and bring it out again at C. Keeping the thread under the needle, insert it again a little to the left on the same level and make a stitch to the centre, remembering to keep the thread under the needle. Repeat these two movements.

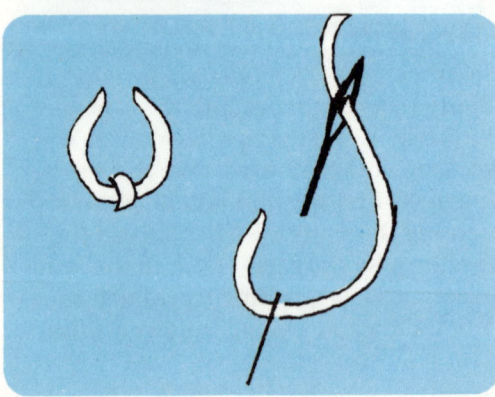

Detached chain stitch

Bring the needle up through the fabric and making a loop with the thread, insert it in nearly the same place. Bring the needle up through the fabric again with the thread under the needle and insert the needle again close to where you have just brought it up.

There are other stitches used in the book, but I have included them where they are used in the text.

Threads and materials

Whether the finished piece of embroidery is to be a delicate or coarse piece of work depends on the combination of threads, materials and stitches. The work will be fine if worked on organdie with two or three strands of stranded cotton, or coarse if worked on burlap, felt or linen with wool [yarn] and Sylko Perle cotton [perle cotton]. The effects that can be achieved by the use of different thicknesses and types of thread have to be practised beforehand and this is dealt with in more detail on page 24.

Thimbles

A thimble should be used in embroidery if possible; in some cases, when one is working with a coarse fabric and thread, a thimble is essential.

Needles

Different types of embroidery require different types of needles. Fine embroidery requires a size 8, 9 or 10 [size 3 to 9] while a size 1 or 2 [size 18 to 24] is used for coarser types of embroidery such as needlepoint and embroidery on net [canvas].

Scissors

A sharp pointed pair of scissors with narrow blades is very important, especially in cut work embroidery when the surplus fabric has to be cut away.

Frames

The finished work will be much neater if the fabric is held taut in a frame, because then the stitches are more likely to be neat and accurate. The beginner will find that an embroidery ring [hoop frame] – consisting of two wooden hoops, one fitting inside the other, with the material

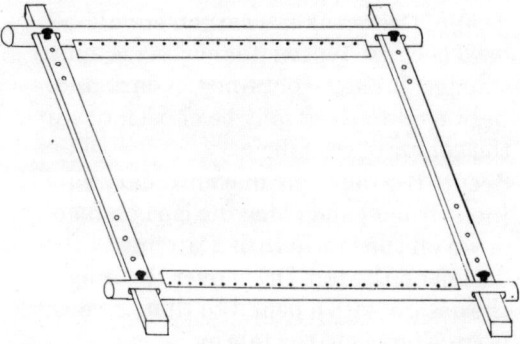

stretched over the inner loop and held in place by the outer loop, which can be adjusted by means of a screw – will suffice for her first attempt.

For more advanced work, the embroidery should be mounted on a square or rectangular frame.

This type of frame usually consists of two rollers, one at the top and one at the bottom, with a wide piece of tape tacked to each roller and a lath on each side fitting into holes on each roller. The material is then stitched on to the tape, the side laths secured with four screws, and the sides of the fabric are laced round the laths with thread.

Transferring the design to the fabric

For those who feel inspired to design their own embroidery, there are several ways of transferring the design to the fabric.

Carbon paper

This is the simplest way of transferring a design. Dressmaker's carbon should be used because typewriter carbon is apt to smudge. It can be obtained in dark and light colours, so it may be chosen to suit the colour of the fabric.

Secure the fabric in an embroidery ring [hoop frame] and place the carbon face down on the fabric with a tracing of the design on the top. Draw over the lines of the design with a pencil so that the design is transferred to the fabric.

Perforating

Trace the design on to a heavy-weight piece of tracing paper and prick holes round the edge of the design with a needle (about $\frac{1}{16}$ in apart). Place the design on the fabric, smooth side upwards, hold in position with weights and rub powdered charcoal or chalk over it, depending on whether the material is dark or light. Remove the tracing paper and, after blowing away the excess powder, paint over the lines with water colour paint.

Direct tracing

If the fabric is fine, for instance organdie, the design may be transferred to the fabric by placing the design underneath the fabric and tracing the lines with a soft pencil or painting them with water colour.

Tacking

This method is used if the fabric is coarse or textured. Trace the design on to tracing paper, tack the paper on to the fabric and sew over the lines with small running stitches. The paper can then be torn away from the material and the tacking removed when the embroidery has been completed.

Detail of Blackwork Apron. For instructions, see page 68

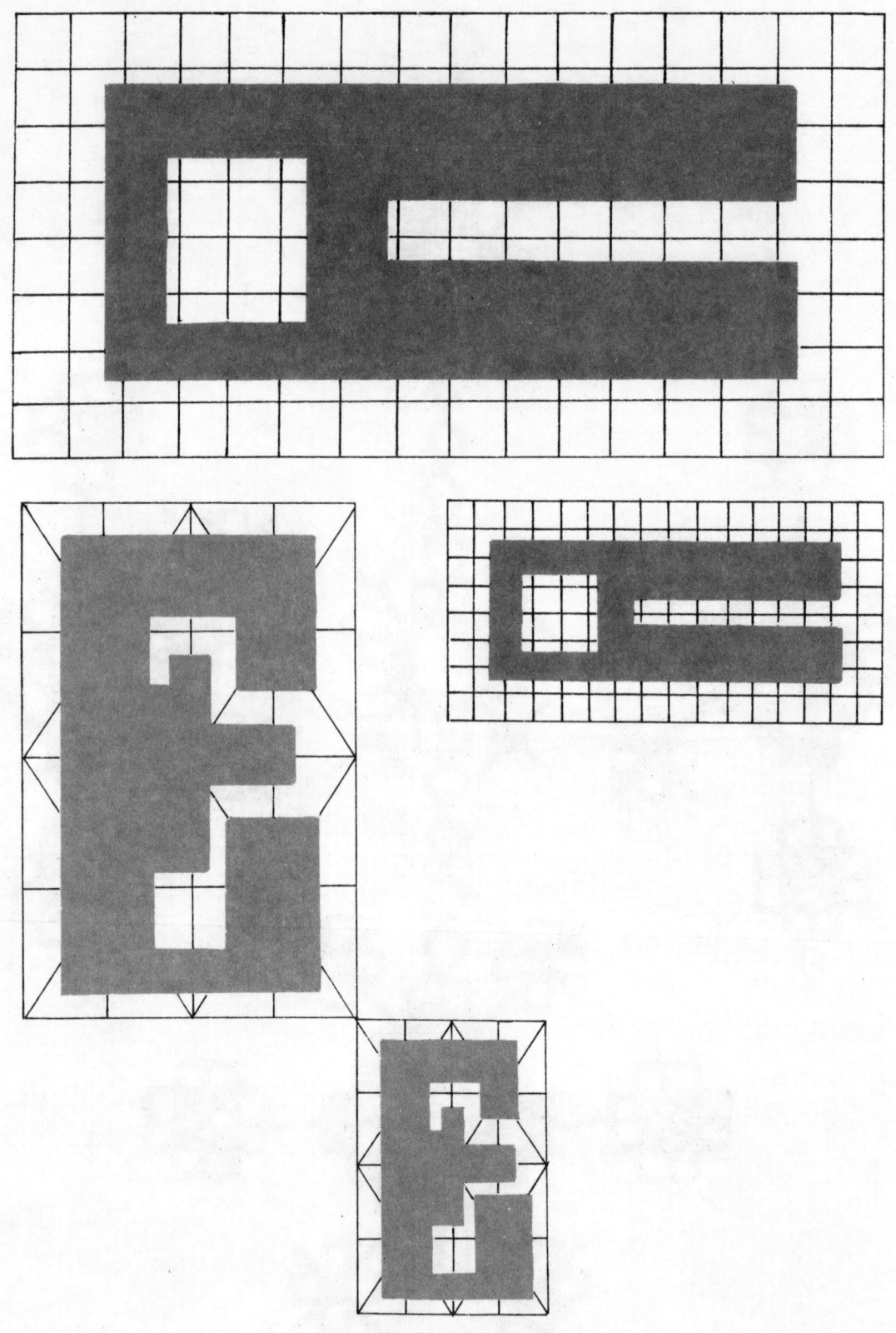

Enlarging and reducing a design

There are several ways of doing this, but I shall only explain the two methods which I think are the easiest. One way to enlarge or reduce a design is to draw $\frac{1}{8}$ in squares over the design to be enlarged and then to draw the corresponding number of squares $\frac{1}{4}$, $\frac{1}{2}$ or 1 in in size and copy the design from the smaller to the large squares.

Another way is to draw a rectangle to fit the design and then to extend one of the diagonals so that it is long enough to form the diagonal of the rectangle of the finished enlargement or reduction. Divide the two rectangles into sections by drawing diagonals to find the centres, then draw diagonals of the quarter sections so that both rectangles can be divided into 16 small rectangles. The design can then be copied from one rectangle to the other.

Mounting finished embroidery

Work a line of tacking [$\frac{1}{4}$ in] stitches around the edge of the finished piece of work, making sure that there is at least 1 in around the edge to turn and stick the embroidery on to the backing.

Cut a piece of strong cardboard the size of the finished picture and stretch the embroidery over it, making sure that the warp and weft threads are kept in line and that the tacking line matches the edge of the cardboard. The piece of work is then glued into place on the wrong side and the corners mitred.

Finally, the picture can be framed, with or without glass, and backed or stuck on to a piece of hardboard.

Three of the methods of embroidery I have used in the book have been in use for many hundreds of years. I have given you a little of the history of these methods along with the instructions because I think that it makes the subject much more interesting.

Patchwork
See diagrams on page 20.
Patchwork reached its height as an art form in the middle of the 18th century, but many years before that it was invented as a means of using up odd pieces of material to make something useful.

The basic method of doing patchwork is fairly simple. First of all, decide on the shapes you want your patches to be (they can be regular or irregular in shape) and try to imagine the colour scheme and the type of fabrics you are going to use.

Trace the shapes on to thin cardboard and cut them out. Place the cardboard shapes on the wrong side of the material, making sure the warp and weft threads are in line. Draw round the outside of the shape with a hard pencil and cut the material $\frac{1}{4}$ in outside the line.

Taking the cardboard shape as a guide, turn the material in $\frac{1}{4}$ in along each edge and tack in position so that the pieces may be sewn together by overcasting along the edges of the shapes. The cardboard pieces can then be removed when the work has been completed.

Patchwork can be further enhanced by using embroidery stitches, such as those shown on the quilt in this book.

There are many traditional combinations of patches such as *flock of geese* and *ninepatch*, which are illustrated. If you are interested in the ancient rather than the modern application of this craft, there are many books available on the subject.

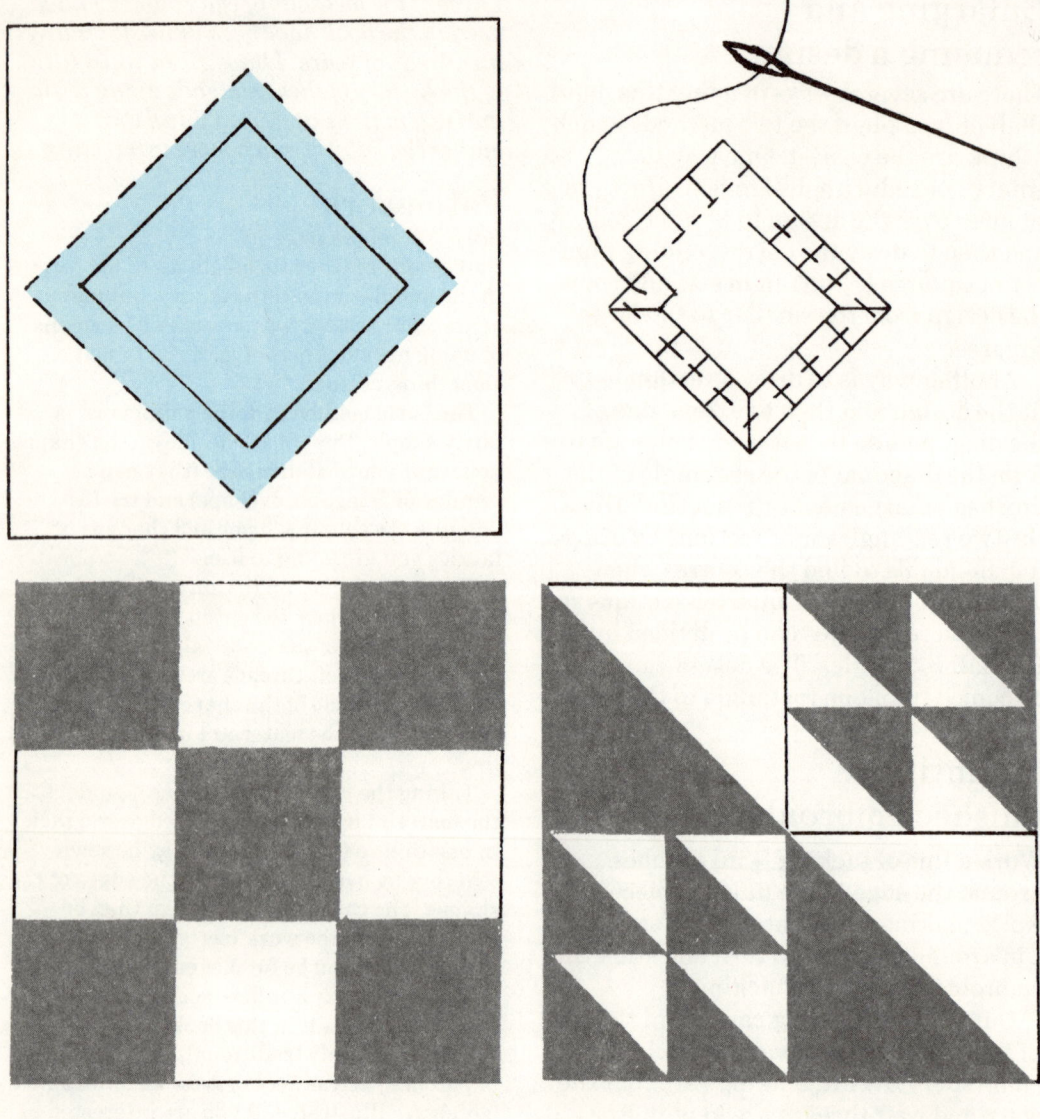

Ninepatch

Flock of geese

Detail from a patchwork quilt, about 1805

Quilting

Originally quilting was used solely for the purpose of making bed covers; its use in Britain dates from the 13th century. It has also been practised for hundreds of years in Europe and countries of the Orient and during the 17th and 18th centuries it was taken over to America by the Dutch and English settlers. In England, quilting became popular as a form of dress embroidery and quilted suits, dresses and petticoats were fashionable during the reigns of Charles I, James I and Queen Anne, in the 17th and 18th centuries. Quilting still survives today in Northumberland and Durham, where it has been handed down from mother to daughter for generations.

Trapunto quilting

Place a layer of silk, satin or fine fabric on top of a layer of wadding which in turn is placed on a piece of muslin marked with the design. Working from the wrong side of the work, sew round the lines of the design through all the layers, using a small running stitch.

Make a small hole in the muslin at the back of each shape to be padded and pad with kapok.

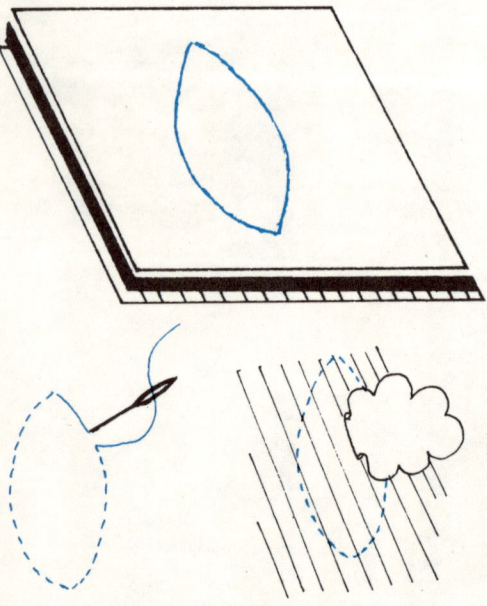

Italian quilting

Three layers of material are used as before. The design is again drawn on the muslin, but this time in double lines $\frac{1}{8}$ in apart.

Working from the wrong side, make a row of small running stitches along each line, then run a cord, padding wool, or heavy yarn between the lines of stitching with a bodkin or large blunt needle. Where there is a curve or corner in the design, bring the needle out of the muslin and make a loop before inserting it again into the muslin.

If desired, the stitching can be done by machine for both these methods of quilting.

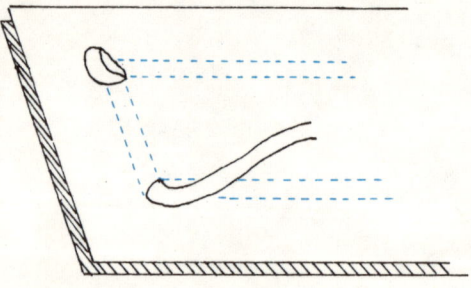

Shadow quilting

This type of quilting is worked in exactly the same way as Italian quilting, but a transparent fabric such as organdie or voile and brightly coloured wool [yarn] are used, so that the colour can be seen through the top layer of material.

Detail from a coverlet of quilted linen, 1703

Appliqué

This is a decorative form of embroidery and its popularity is due to the fact that almost any type of material can be used for the background and shapes. Pieces of fabric are stitched in place on the background material and stitches can be used to enhance the design. In many cases, however, the appliqué needs no decoration at all.

The type of material chosen must be suitable for the use to which the finished article is to be put. With household articles it should be remembered that the material appliquéd will have to be washable, so a fabric such as cotton is often very suitable. For pictures, linen, velvet, silk and woollen materials may be used.

The design should be marked on the background fabric and the shapes to be appliquéd should be traced on to thin cardboard. Mark the shape on the fabric in the same way as for patchwork, leaving $\frac{1}{4}$ in turning around the edge.

Cut the shape out along the outer edge and tack the $\frac{1}{4}$ in turning in place on the wrong side of the shape. The piece can then be machine stitched or slip stitched in place on the design, using a matching or contrasting thread. For quick and effective results, felt may be appliquéd. This is especially useful for wall hangings and cushion covers where it can simply be tacked in place without having to turn in the edges.

Appliqué is also finding a use in collage; it is stuck, rather than sewn in place.

Use of stitches

As I have already mentioned, many different effects can be achieved by combining different types of threads. A good exercise for anyone attempting embroidery for the first time is to draw a four inch circle on a piece of linen and mount it in a circular frame, so that you can try out various stitches.

Working from the outside of the circle, work two foundation [initial] rows of straight stitches in Sylko Perle cotton [perle cotton] in preparation for the raised chain band stitch. Work the chain band in wool, then work one row of straight stitches in wool and the chain band in Sylko Perle cotton [perle cotton].

Threaded backstitch can then be worked by sewing a row of backstitch in Sylko Perle cotton [perle cotton], then threading this with wool [yarn] or stranded cotton with the same colour running both ways.

Chain stitch, knot stitch, fly stitch and French knots all make for variety when worked in different types of thread. Spider's webs can be chunky when the foundation stitches are worked in Sylko Perle [perle cotton] and the back stitches in wool, or finer if worked the other way round: thick wool [yarn], couched in place with Sylko Perle cotton [perle cotton].

As you continue to experiment, you will find that the effects of string, raffia and of threads pulled from material all help to make your embroidery much more exciting and original – which is, after all, the aim of the embroidress.

Embroidery in the home

Binca needlework bag

Materials

½ yd moss green Binca or Panama canvas,
42 ins wide, six squares to 1 in
Clarks' Anchor Stranded cotton [Coats Six
Strand Floss], two skeins flame red, two
skeins medium turquoise and two skeins
white. Use six strands of cotton throughout
One pair of wooden sewing bag handles,
13 ins wide
One no. 21 tapestry needle

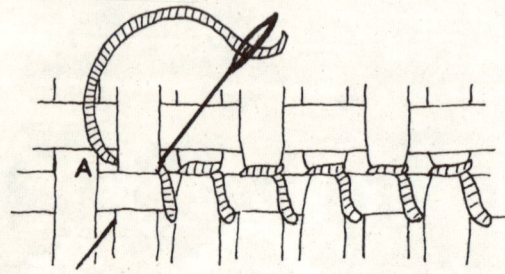

for colour illustration, see previous
page

Working instructions

There are only two stitches used, cross stitch
and hem stitch.

Cross stitch

Work this stitch as for ordinary cross stitch,
but take the thread over one group of threads
in each direction.

Hem stitch

To work the hem stitch which attaches the
bag to the handles, turn 1½ in of the hem to
the wrong side, through the gap in the bag
handles. Keeping the threads of the fabric
even, fasten the red stranded cotton ½ in from
the bottom of the hem on the right hand side.
Bring it through to the right side of the fabric
at A and complete the stitch as shown in the
diagram.
    To start work, cut two pieces of Binca 20 ins
wide and 17 ins deep, 2 ins bigger all round
than the finished size of 16 × 13 ins, so that it
will not matter if the edges of the fabric fray
slightly when working.
    Commencing at the right hand corner,
2 ins away from each edge of the fabric, work
the complete motif given in the diagram in
cross stitch, then repeat it twice more.
    Take the smaller motif and work it in the
two spaces left between the large motifs, but
with white crosses in the centre instead of red.
    To make up the bag, trim the Binca canvas
to the finished size plus an extra ½ in seam
allowance and 1½ in hem allowance. Place
the two right sides together and machine
stitch ½ in away from the edges, leaving the
top open. Sew the top of the bag to the handles
as explained in the instructions for the hem
stitch.

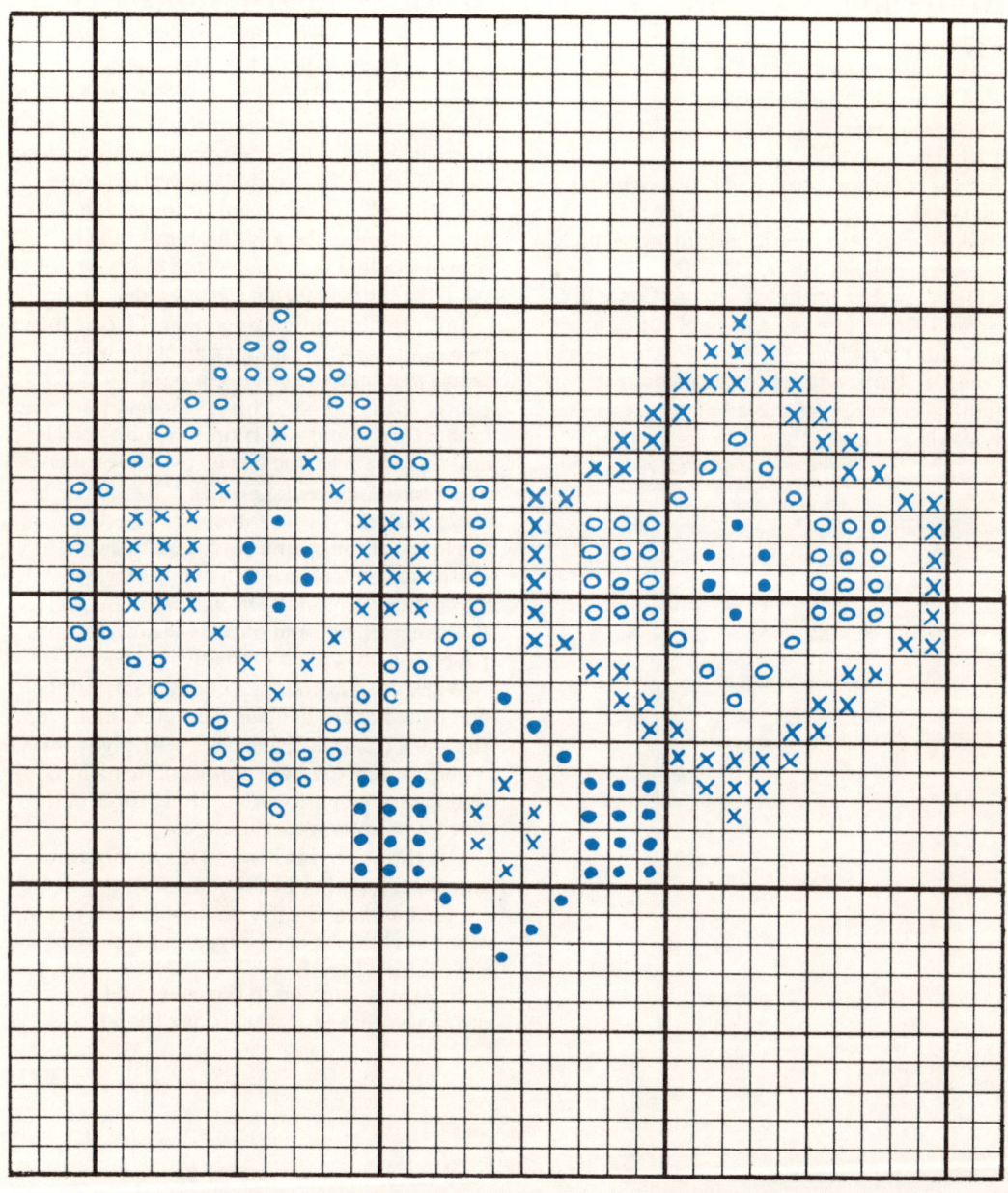

Cushion cover

Materials

½ yd 36 ins wide brown and white furnishing [upholstery] fabric
½ yd 36 ins wide calico cotton
⅜ yd cream net
¼ yd brown net
Scraps of cream cotton and brown woollen material
Sylko Perle cotton [perle cotton], no. 8 thickness, one ball each of nos. 803, 806
Clarks' Anchor Stranded cotton [Coats Six Strand Floss], one skein each of coffee brown and pale cinnamon
One reel [ball] of dark brown and one reel [ball] of cream Sylko thread
A 1 lb bag of kapok

Working instructions

Draw a 10 ins circle, a $6\frac{1}{2}$ ins circle, a 5 ins circle, a 4 ins circle and a $2\frac{1}{2}$ ins circle. Following the diagram, cut the four holes in the outer circle and cut out the largest circle in cream net; the $6\frac{1}{2}$ ins circle in cream cotton; the 5 ins circle in two thicknesses of brown net, with a $2\frac{1}{2}$ ins circle cut in the middle, slightly to one side; and the 4 ins circle in brown woollen material with a $2\frac{1}{2}$ ins circle cut from the centre, also to one side.

Cut the furnishing [upholstery] fabric into two 18 ins lengths, mount one of these in a frame and tack the circles in position in the centre of the square. Thread the machine with cream thread and sew round the large circle and the cream cotton circle, five times each. Machine stitch round circles a, b and c three times with the cream cotton.

Thread the machine with dark brown cotton and machine stitch round circle d three times, round the brown woollen circle five times (inside and outside the circle) and round the brown net circle five times.

Work the rows of open chain, back stitch and raised chain band as indicated. Remove the work from the frame and, with right sides together, sew the two squares of furnishing upholstery fabric together along three of the sides, $\frac{1}{2}$ in away from the edge.

Cut the calico into two 18 ins squares and sew them together in the same way as you did for the cushion. Stuff with kapok, turn in $\frac{1}{2}$ in along each of the open edges and slip stitch the cushion together.

Insert the cushion in the cover and slip stitch the cover together along the edge.

Cushion cover

Stranded cotton
3 *pale cinnamon, open chain and backstitch*
1 *coffee brown, open chain and backstitch*
4 *coffee brown, backstitch*
ooo*raised chain band with 803 as foundation*
stitches and pale cinnamon as the top row

Sylko Perle cotton
5 *803, open chain and backstitch*
2 *806, open chain and backstitch*

Machine stitching
E *dark brown machine stitching*
F *cream machine stitching*

Stitches
ooo*raised chain band*
- - -*backstitch*

Machine embroidered wastepaper bin

Materials

One tin, $7\frac{1}{4}$ ins tall and $5\frac{1}{2}$ ins diameter
A rectangle of blue linen-type fabric $8\frac{1}{4} \times 19$ ins
Scraps of felt in light, medium and dark pink
Eight large pink wooden beads
One skein each of Clark's Anchor Stranded cotton [Coats Six Strand Floss], in lilac, mauve-pink, medium dusty pink and deep pink
Reels [balls] of Sylko cotton in black, pale and dark pink and blue to match the material.

Working instructions

To enlarge the diagram, cut a piece of paper 10 ins square and divide into 1 in squares. Copy the design on to this.

Trace the design on to tracing paper and place it on the right side of the material, $1\frac{3}{4}$ ins away from the side of the rectangle and $\frac{1}{2}$ in away from the top and bottom edges, with a piece of carbon face down on the material under the tracing paper. Draw over the lines, keeping the tracing paper firmly in position so that the design is transferred to the fabric. Repeat the process $1\frac{1}{4}$ in away from the other side of the rectangle, remembering to reverse the tracing paper so that the design is transferred the other way round.

Remove the presser foot from the machine and lower the 'drop feed'. Mount the fabric in a 7 ins diameter embroidery frame so that the first design to be worked is held tightly in the centre.

Using the tracing as a pattern, cut out the felt in three shades of pink as shown on the diagram and machine stitch in place with pale pink cotton. Thread the machine with dark pink cotton and place the embroidery ring under the needle. Work three rows of stitching along the four upright lines of the design and then, moving the ring backwards and forwards, fill in the top two circles on the left hand side and the bottom three circles on the right hand side.

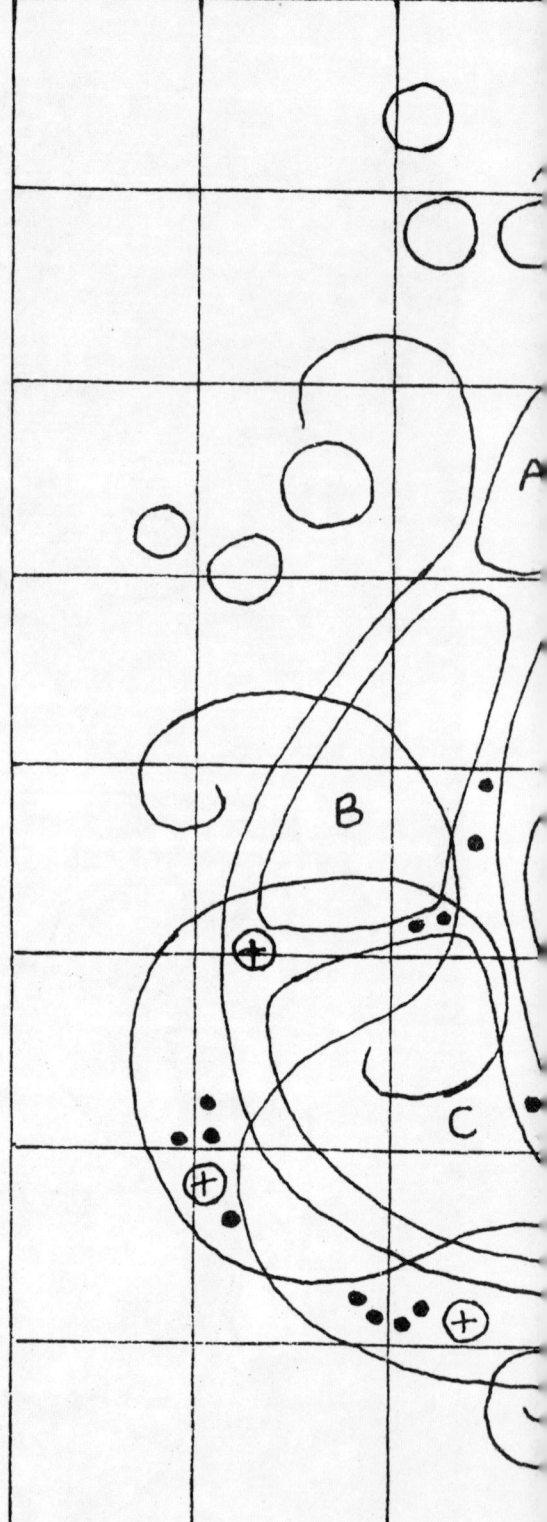

Thread the machine with pale pink cotton, then work one line of stitching near each of the three pink ones you have just worked, one for each of the lower lines, and fill in the rest of the circles.

Thread the machine with black cotton and work a line of stitching next to each of the pale pink lines and another line next to – but not quite as long as – each of the four upright lines. Finish off the black stitching by machine stitching a single line around one of each of the four groups of circles.

Repeat this for the other side, working the top two circles on the right hand side and the bottom three on the left hand side in dark pink cotton and the rest in pale pink cotton.

Stitch the beads in place as indicated with stranded cotton, using three strands and taking six or eight stitches through the centre of each bead. Finish off the embroidery by working clusters of French knots in the two shades of pink stranded cotton using six strands. Repeat this for the other design as well and, with the right sides together, machine stitch along the shorter edge taking a $\frac{1}{2}$ in seam allowance. Turn a single $\frac{1}{2}$ in hem to the wrong side along the top and bottom edges and herringbone in position.

A *pale pink felt*
B *medium pink felt*
C *dark pink felt*
• *clusters of French knots*
⊕ *pink wooden beads*

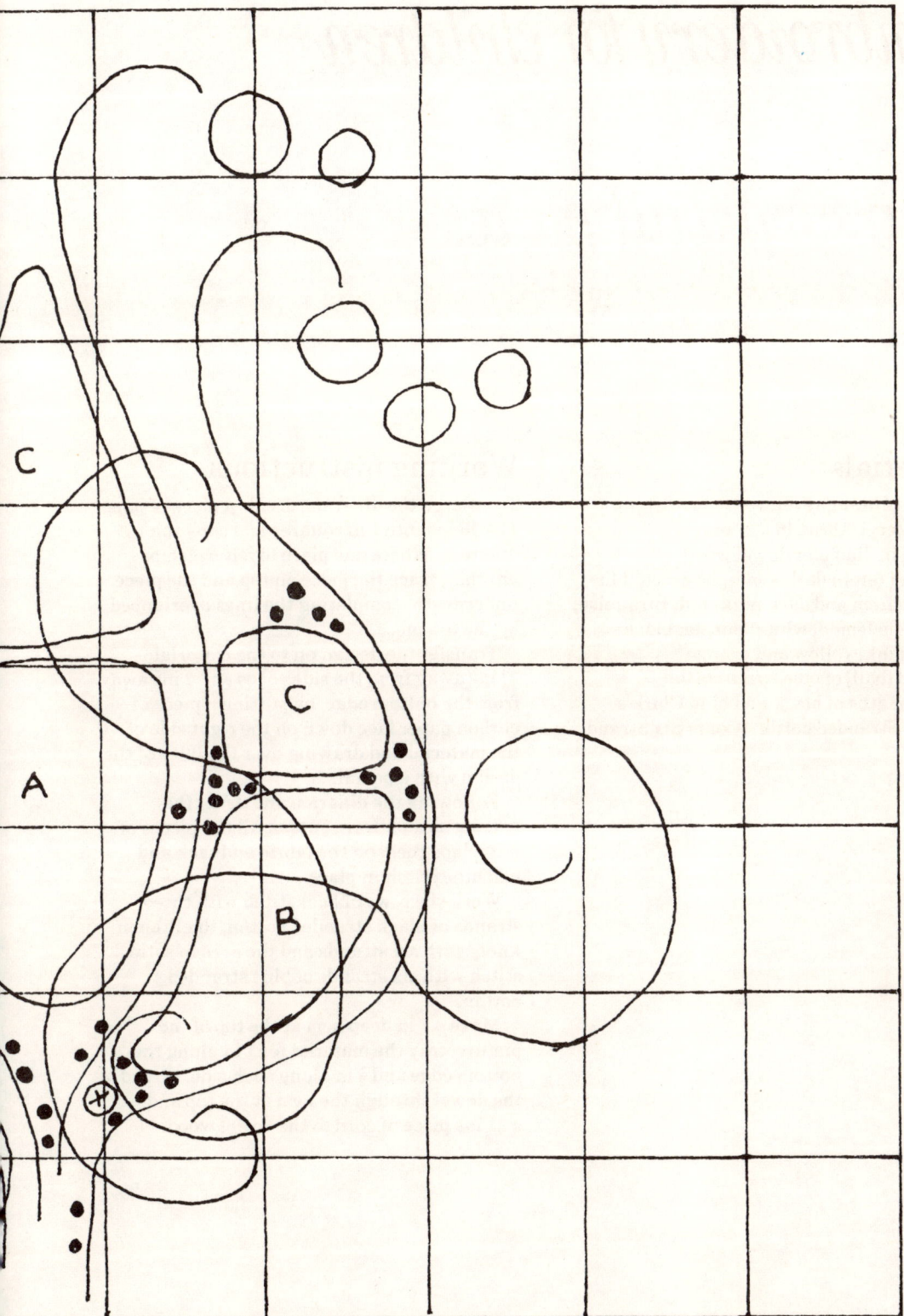

Embroidery for children

Nursery wall panel

Materials

A piece of orange evenweave furnishing
[upholstery] fabric, 16 × 22 ins
$\frac{1}{2}$ yd of $\frac{1}{2}$ in diameter dowel wood
Scraps of felt in dark and light green; blue;
pale, medium and dark pink; red; turquoise;
fawn; pale lemon; white; purple; black;
mauve/pink; yellow and orange
One reel [ball] of blue Sylko cotton
Short lengths of black and blue Clark's
Anchor Stranded cotton [Coats Six Strand
Floss]

Working instructions

To enlarge the diagram, divide a piece of paper
11 × 16 ins into 1 in squares and copy the
diagram. Where one piece of felt overlaps
another, trace the piece on top and the piece
underneath, completing the lines overlapped
by the top piece.

Transfer the design on to the material,
$2\frac{3}{4}$ ins away from the side edges and 2 ins away
from the bottom edge, by putting a piece of
carbon paper face down on the right side of
the material and drawing over the lines of the
design with a pencil.

Following the diagram and using the
tracing as a pattern, cut out all the pieces of
felt, place them on the fabric and tack and
machine stitch in place.

Work the rows of backstitch with three
strands of black stranded cotton, the French
knots with six strands and the eyes in satin
stitch with six strands of blue stranded
cotton.

Make a 1 in deep hem at the top of the
picture, fray the material for 1 in along the
bottom edge and $\frac{1}{2}$ in along each side, thread
the dowel through the hem at the top and tie
a 21 ins piece of cord to the dowel wood.

a	*pale green felt*	e	*medium pink felt*	i	*fawn felt*	n	*black felt*
b	*dark green felt*	f	*dark pink felt*	k	*pale lemon felt*	o	*mauve/pink felt*
c	*blue felt*	g	*red felt*	l	*white felt*	p	*yellow felt*
d	*pale pink felt*	h	*turquoise felt*	m	*purple felt*	q	*orange felt*

Embroidered patchwork pram cover

Materials

$\frac{1}{2}$ yd 36 ins wide pink lining material
$\frac{1}{2}$ yd 36 ins wide mauve cotton lawn
$\frac{1}{2}$ yd 36 ins wide cotton wadding
Scraps of material for the patches in pink, orange, red and patterned cotton
Clark's Anchor Stranded cotton [Coats Six Strand Floss], one skein each of Wedgwood blue, medium dark blue, emerald, bright canary yellow and wine-mauve
One sheet of thin card

for colour illustration, see page 41
for diagram, see overleaf

Working instructions

Draw a piece of paper 16 × 24 ins into 1 in squares and copy the diagram. Trace the shapes on to the thin card and cut them out. Place the shapes on the wrong side of the material and cut out the shapes, allowing $\frac{1}{4}$ in extra all the way round.

Tack the material to the card along the edges, the right side of the material facing upwards. Do this with all the pieces of material and then oversew [overcast] them together along the edges.

Remove the pieces of card and work the fly stitch, French knots, feather stitch, backstitch and threaded backstitch as indicated.

Cut five $3\frac{1}{2}$ ins wide strips on the cross from the mauve cotton and sew them all together. Machine stitch a $\frac{1}{2}$ in hem along one edge and gather the other $\frac{1}{2}$ in away from the edge.

Cut a rectangle of pink lining material 24 × 17 ins and a rectangle of wadding 23 × 16 ins. Turn under $\frac{1}{2}$ in all the way round the edge of the patchwork, draw up the frill to fit around the edge and tack in place, with the right side of the frill to the wrong side of the patchwork. Lay the piece of wadding on the wrong side of the patchwork and tack in place.

Turn in $\frac{1}{2}$ in along the edges of the lining material and tack it to the back of the patchwork along the edges.

Machine stitch all the thicknesses together $\frac{1}{8}$ in away from the edge of the patchwork on the right side. Remove all the tacking stitches.

— *dark emerald, feather stitch*
← *wedgwood blue, single row of fly stitch*
⚡ *medium dark blue, double row of fly stitch, dark blue on the outside and pale blue on the inside*

--- *dark emerald, backstitch*
-ooo- *backstitch threaded with bright canary yellow and wine-mauve*
• *medium dark blue, French knots*

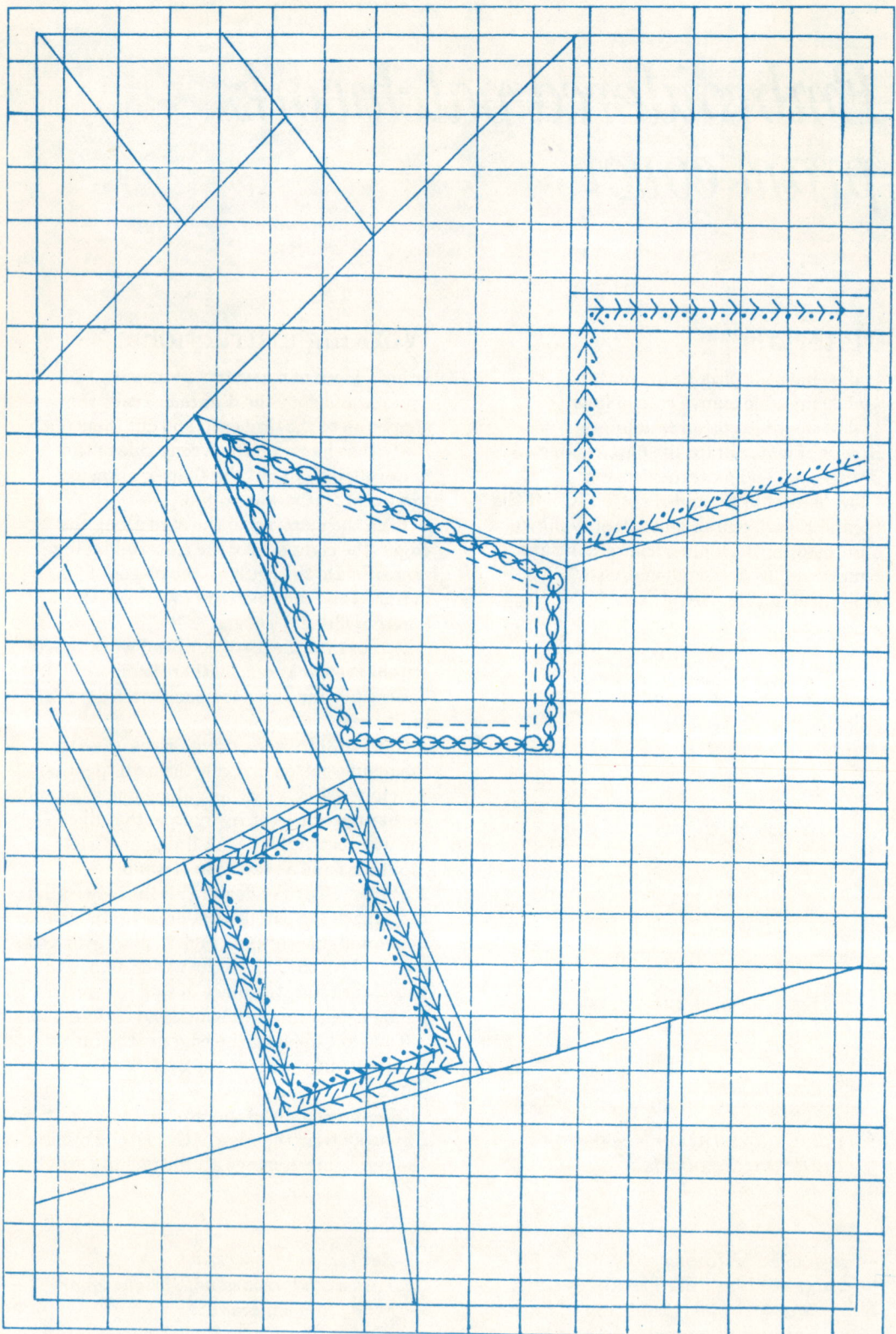

Child's smocked sun hat

Materials

$\frac{1}{4}$ yd 36 ins wide cotton material with a firm weave
Clark's Anchor Stranded cotton [Coats Six Strand Floss], one skein each of pale peach, gold and mint green
Transfer for smocking dots, $\frac{1}{4}$ in apart
Use six strands of cotton throughout

Working instructions

Cut a rectangle of cotton material $4\frac{1}{2} \times 28$ ins.
Cut a strip from the smocking dot transfer $27 \times 1\frac{3}{4}$ ins and stamp on to the wrong side of the material, $\frac{1}{2}$ in away from one of the long edges.
Gather the first row of dots as shown in the diagram and pull the gathers up so that they measure 10 ins.

Smocking stitches

Work the rows of smocking as explained below, using the stitch diagrams and the diagrammatic section of the finished piece of smocking to help you.

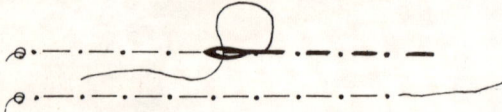

Cable stitch (rows 1,6 and 7)
see diagrams overleaf

Make a knot in the cotton and bring the needle through on the left of the material between the first two dots, i.e. the first fold. Insert the needle again taking in a gather and bring it through the first dot, i.e. take a stitch through the fold at right angles to it. Keeping the thread below the needle, pick up a gather and pull the thread upwards. Then, keeping the thread above the needle, pick up another gather and pull the thread downwards.

Continue in this way until you reach the end of the row.

One-step wave stitch (rows 2,3,4 and 5)
see diagrams overleaf

Following diagram 1, work five stitches in cable stitch. Then, with the thread below the needle pick up the next gather ($\frac{1}{2}$ a step up) and pull the needle upwards (diagram 1).

for colour illustration, see page 45

With the thread above the needle, pick up the next gather and pull the thread down (diagram 2). With the thread still above the needle, pick up the next gather ($\frac{1}{2}$ step down) and pull the needle down (diagram 3).

Finally, with the thread below the needle,

To make up the hat, cut a strip of material 10×3 ins. With the right sides together, machine stitch the strip to the first row of gathers of the smocking, taking a $\frac{1}{2}$ in seam. Fold the smocking in half lengthwise and stitch together $\frac{1}{2}$ in away from the edge.

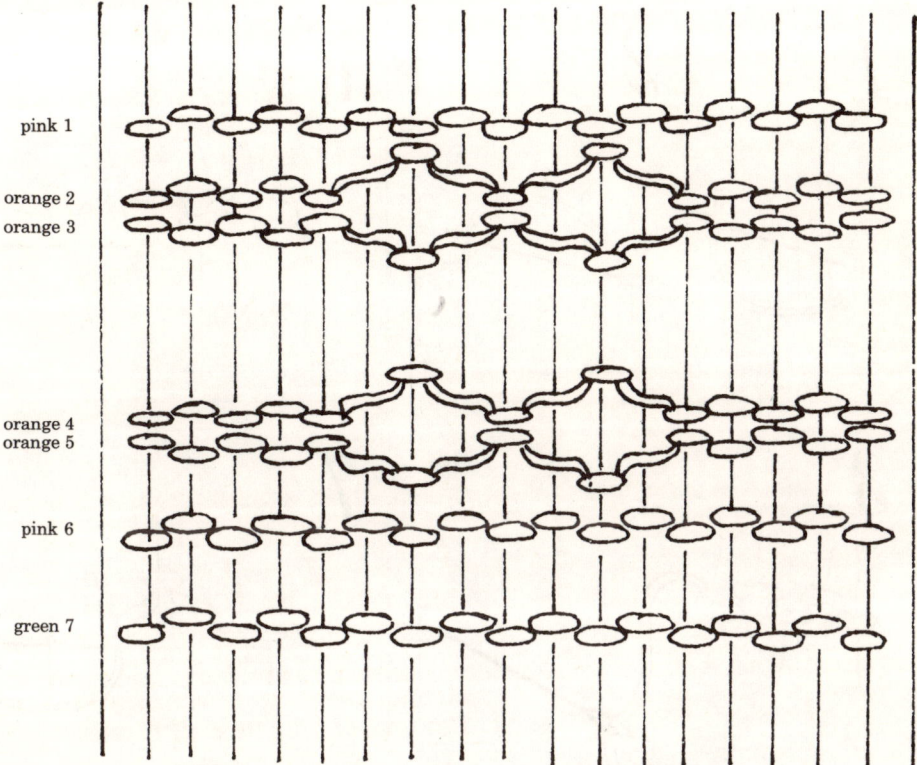

pink 1

orange 2
orange 3

orange 4
orange 5

pink 6

green 7

pick up the next gather and pull the needle upwards (diagram 4).

Continue by working another one-step wave stitch (diagram 5), five cable stitches and two one-step wave stitches, etc. until the end of the row, ending with five cable stitches.

Rows 3 and 5 are worked in the same way, but the position of the thread is reversed, i.e. when the thread is under the needle in rows 2 and 4 it is above the needle in rows 3 and 5, and when it is above the needle in rows 2 and 4 it is below the needle in rows 3 and 5.

Machine stitch a $\frac{1}{4}$ in hem along the edge of the piece of material that you did the smocking on.

Turn to the wrong side and gather the edge of the strip of material that you sewed on to the smocking, $\frac{1}{2}$ in away from the edge, and draw up as tightly as possible. Turn the hat to the right side.

Cut two strips of material 14×1 ins. Fold in half lengthwise, wrong sides together along the long edges, taking a $\frac{1}{8}$ in turning. Stitch the two ties to the hat half way between the back seam and front foldline.

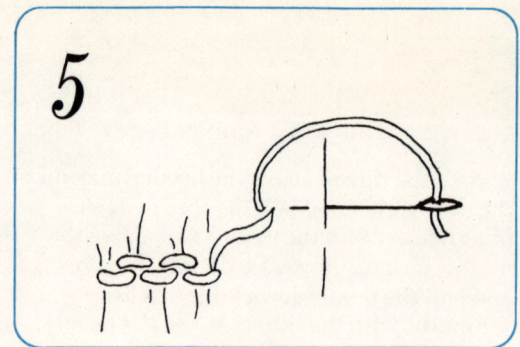

5

1 **2**

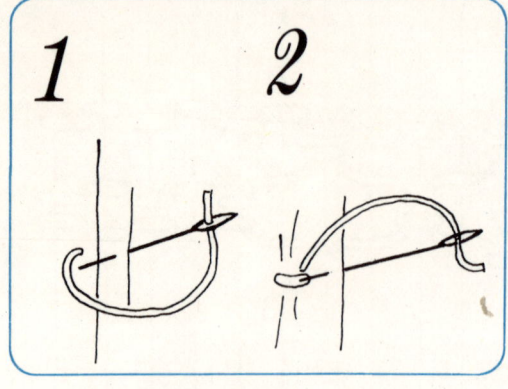

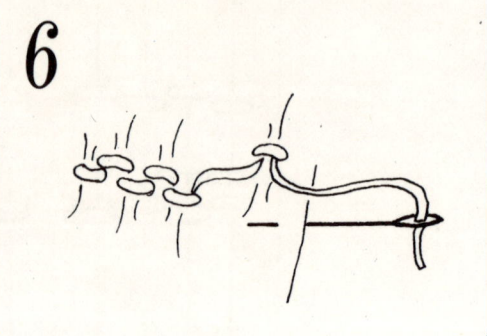

6

3

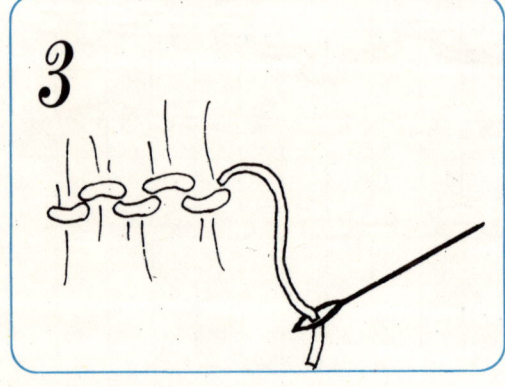

7

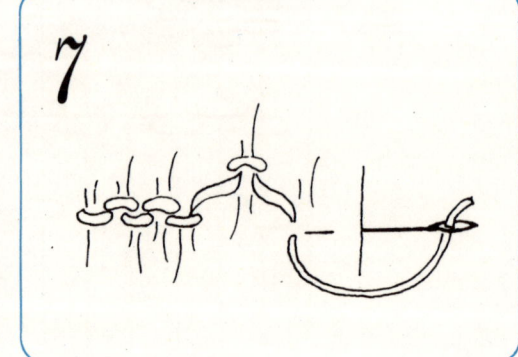

4

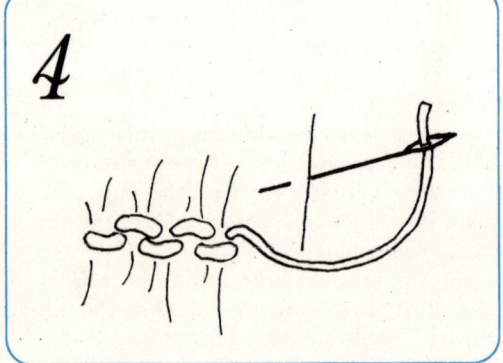

8

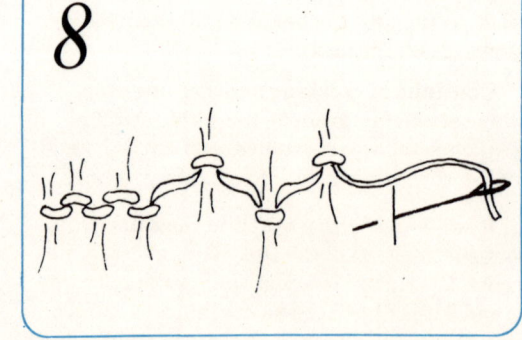

Embroidered felt ball

Materials

One 12 ins square of mauve felt and one 12 ins square of yellow felt
8 oz of kapok
One ball each of Sylko Perle cotton [perle cotton] no. 8 thickness, nos. 706, 744 and 924

for colour illustration, see page 9

† 0229, backstitch
⪪ 706, fly stitch and satin stitch
Υ 0229, fly stitch
• 706, French knots
● 774, French knots
◊ 706, satin stitch and 0229 lazy daisy stitch
♀ 706 satin stitch and 0229 French knot

Working instructions

To enlarge the diagram of one of the sections of the ball, cut a piece of paper 10 × 3 ins, divide into 1 in squares and copy the diagram. Then, using the pattern as a guide, cut four mauve and four yellow sections in felt. Trace the main lines of the working diagram, i.e. the three circles and the lines of backstitch and flystitch, on tracing paper and transfer them on to the mauve felt by putting carbon paper face down on the felt and drawing over the lines of the design with a pencil.

Mount a 14 × 12 ins piece of muslin in a slate frame and tack the pieces of felt on to the muslin.

To embroider a section of the ball, cut out three yellow felt circles, pad gently with kapok and oversew [overcast] into position. Work the lines you have transferred on to the felt in fly stitch and backstitch; then, using the working diagram as a guide, work the French knots, satin stitches and single lazy daisy stitches around the edges of the circles and the French knots between the fly stitching.

When you have embroidered all the sections, take them out of the frame and trim away the excess muslin as close to the wrong side of the embroidery as possible. Taking one mauve and one yellow section alternately, oversew [overcast] all the sections together leaving the last seam open.

Cut three strips of yellow felt $\frac{1}{4}$ in wide and 12 ins long, plait [braid] them, knot them at both ends and insert one of the knotted ends the top of the ball and sew in position. Leave a 3 ins gap in the seam and stuff the ball firmly with kapok.

Finish sewing up the seam, cut a $1\frac{1}{2}$ in circle from the yellow felt and oversew [overcast] it to the bottom of the ball.

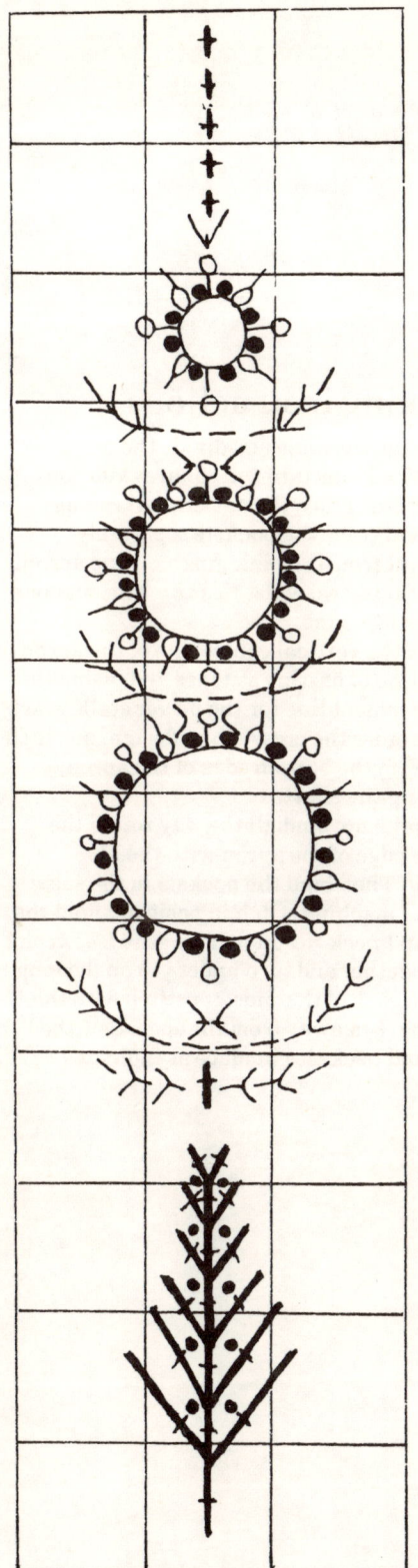

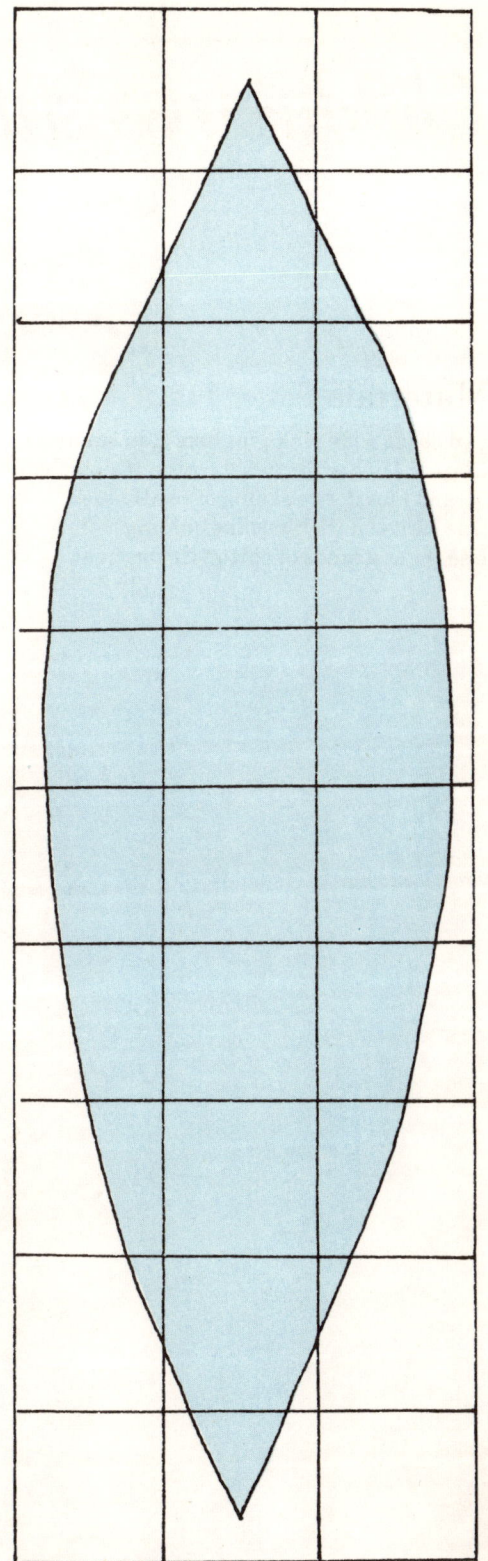

Child's cross stitch apron

Materials

$\frac{1}{2}$ yd 36 ins wide pink gingham ($\frac{1}{4}$ in squares)
Clark's Anchor Stranded cotton [Coats Six Strand Floss], two skeins of royal blue
One card of dark blue bias binding
Use three strands of cotton throughout

Working instructions

To enlarge the diagram, divide the piece of paper 15 × 17 ins into 1 in squares and copy the pattern. Trace the pattern on tracing paper and trace the pockets separately.

Cut out from the pink gingham one apron, two pockets, two waist ties 18 × 3 ins and one neck tie 16 × 3 ins.

Mark the vertical centre line of the apron with a line of basting stitches and, using this as a placement line for the flower stalk, start to embroider the cross stitch design, one inch away from the bottom edge of the apron, following the chart.

To make up, bind all the way round the outside edge of the apron with the blue binding. Then bind the pockets in the same way and machine stitch in position. Fold the waist and neck ties in half lengthwise, wrong sides together and turn under $\frac{1}{2}$ in on the long side and each of the ends; topstitch with the machine, $\frac{1}{8}$ in away from the edge. Sew the waist and neck ties in place as indicated.

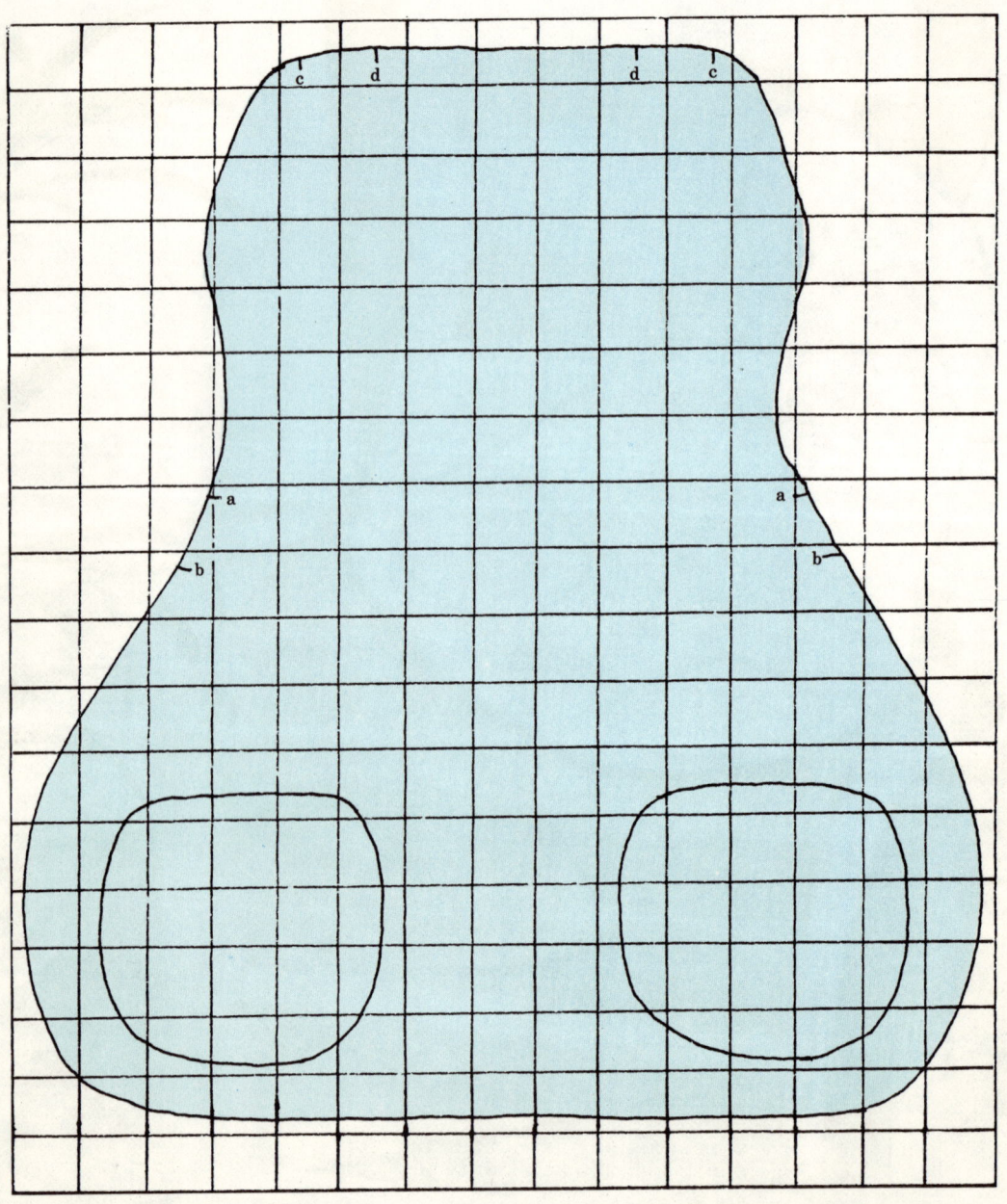

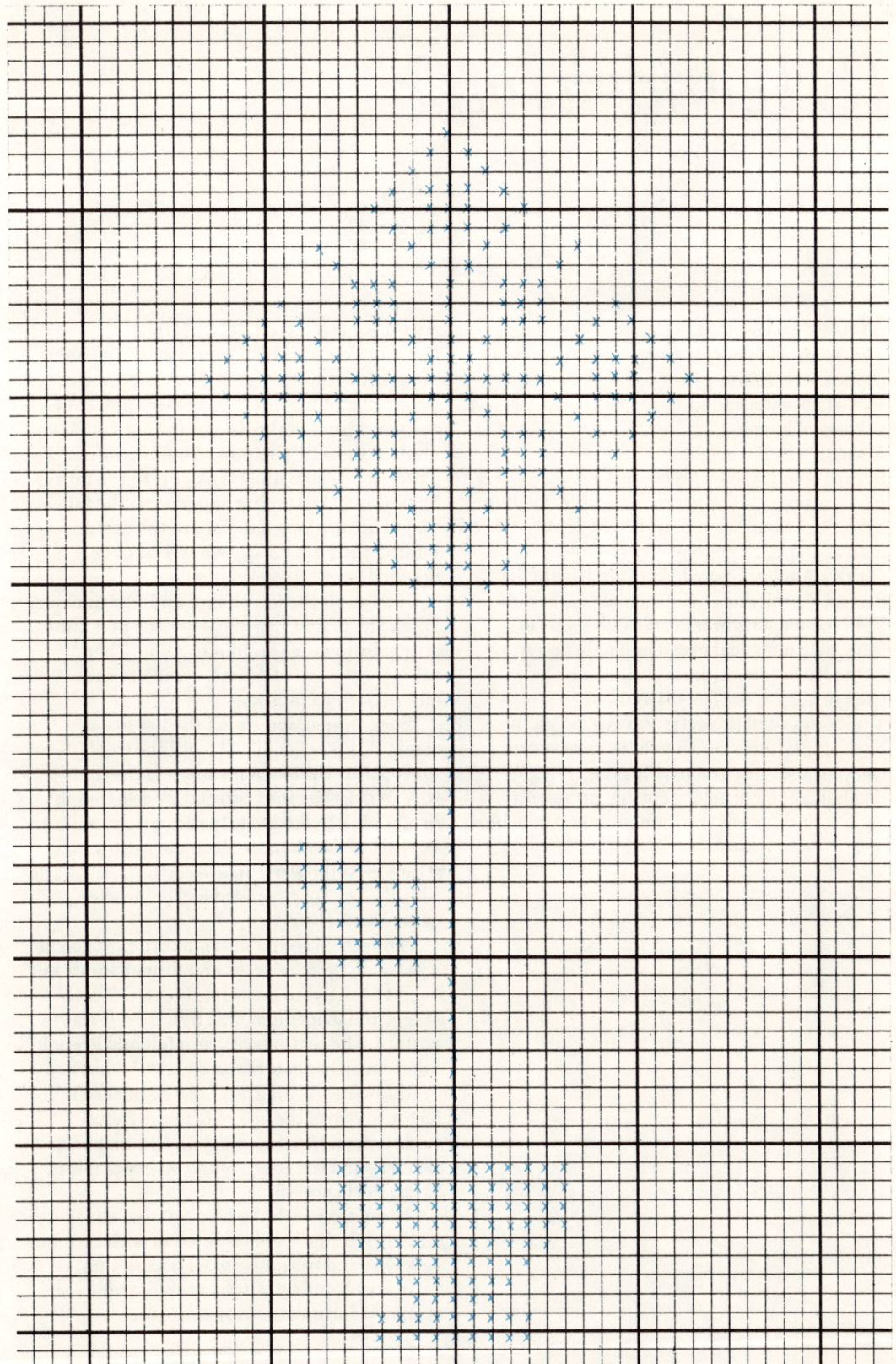

Owl cushion cover

Materials

½ yd 36 ins wide purple evenweave furnishing [upholstery] fabric
½ yd 36 ins wide calico
1 lb bag of kapok
Matching Sylko cotton
Scraps of felt in pale green, leaf green, medium green, dark green, pale blue, medium blue, dark blue, turquoise, bright pink, dark mauve and light mauve
Clark's Anchor Stranded cotton [Coats Six Strand Floss], one skein each of bright pink, light mauve, bright jade, medium powder blue, pale blue, leaf green and pale green
Sylko Perle cotton [perle cotton], one ball each of nos.26,769,746,924 and 746
Tapisserie wool [tapestry yarn], one skein each of turquoise, medium blue, lime green, medium and dark green, pale green
Anchor soft embroidery cotton, one skein each of dark green, medium pink and pale blue

Working instructions

Cut an 18 ins square of purple material and mount it in a slate frame. Divide a piece of paper 12 × 14 ins into 1 in squares and copy the main lines of the design so that you have enough lines to give you a rough outline. Trace the design and transfer it to the fabric by pinning the tracing paper on to the fabric and tacking along the lines of the design, pulling the paper away when you have finished.

Cut out all the felt shapes and sew in place. Work the main lines of backstitch and knot stitch, following the colour guide. Then, taking a section at a time, complete the embroidery as follows:

Work the section round the left eye in straight lines of couched pale blue wool [yarn] and outline the two felt shapes in the same way. Work the other two couched shapes in bright pink Sylko Perle [perle cotton]. Fill in the rest of the shape with single satin and fly stitch in Sylko Perle [perle cotton] no.769 and Clark's Anchor Stranded cotton no.0189, using three strands.

The section round the right eye can then be worked in Spiders' webs and French knots in bright pink Sylko Perle [perle cotton], and star stitch in medium pink Sylko Perle [perle cotton]. The sections of green felt and French knots on either side of the owl can be worked by following the diagram, adding backstitch on top of two of the pieces of felt in Sylko Perle cotton [perle cotton] no.924, and backstitch round the edges of the pieces of felt in Sylko Perle no.746.

The section with the blue felt and stitchery on the right hand side is filled in with couched pale blue and turquoise wool [yarn], single satin stitch and fly stitch in three strands of stranded cotton nos. 0244 and 0254.

To make up the cushion cover, take the other square of purple fabric and with the right sides together, machine stitch $\frac{1}{2}$ in away from the edge on three of the sides. Cut two 18 ins squares of calico and sew them together in the same way. Stuff the calico cover with the kapok and slipstitch the open side together as before, taking in a $\frac{1}{2}$ in turning.

Felt

A$_1$ *pale green*
A$_2$ *leaf green*
A$_3$ *medium green*
A$_4$ *dark green*
B$_1$ *pale blue*
B$_2$ *medium blue*
B$_3$ *dark blue*
B$_4$ *turquoise*
X   *bright pink*
Y   *dark mauve*
Z   *light mauve*

Stranded cotton

1   *bright pink*
2   *light mauve*
3   *bright jade green*
4   *pale blue*
5   *medium powder blue*
6   *leaf green*
7   *pale green*

Anchor soft embroidery cotton

9   *medium green*
10   *medium pink*
11   *pale blue*

Sylko Perle cotton

A   *26*
B   *769*
C   *746*
D   *924*

Wool

8   *lime green*

Stitches

– – – *backstitch*
 Y *flystitch*
+++ *couching*
 * *star stitch*
 — *satin stitch*
ooo *knot stitch*
 ● *Spiders web filling*

French knots

O *medium green*
● *dark green*   } *wool*
⊙ *lime green*
✦ *pale green*

 • *medium green* } *soft embroidery*
o *dark green*   } *cotton*
⊕ *no.26 Sylko Perle*

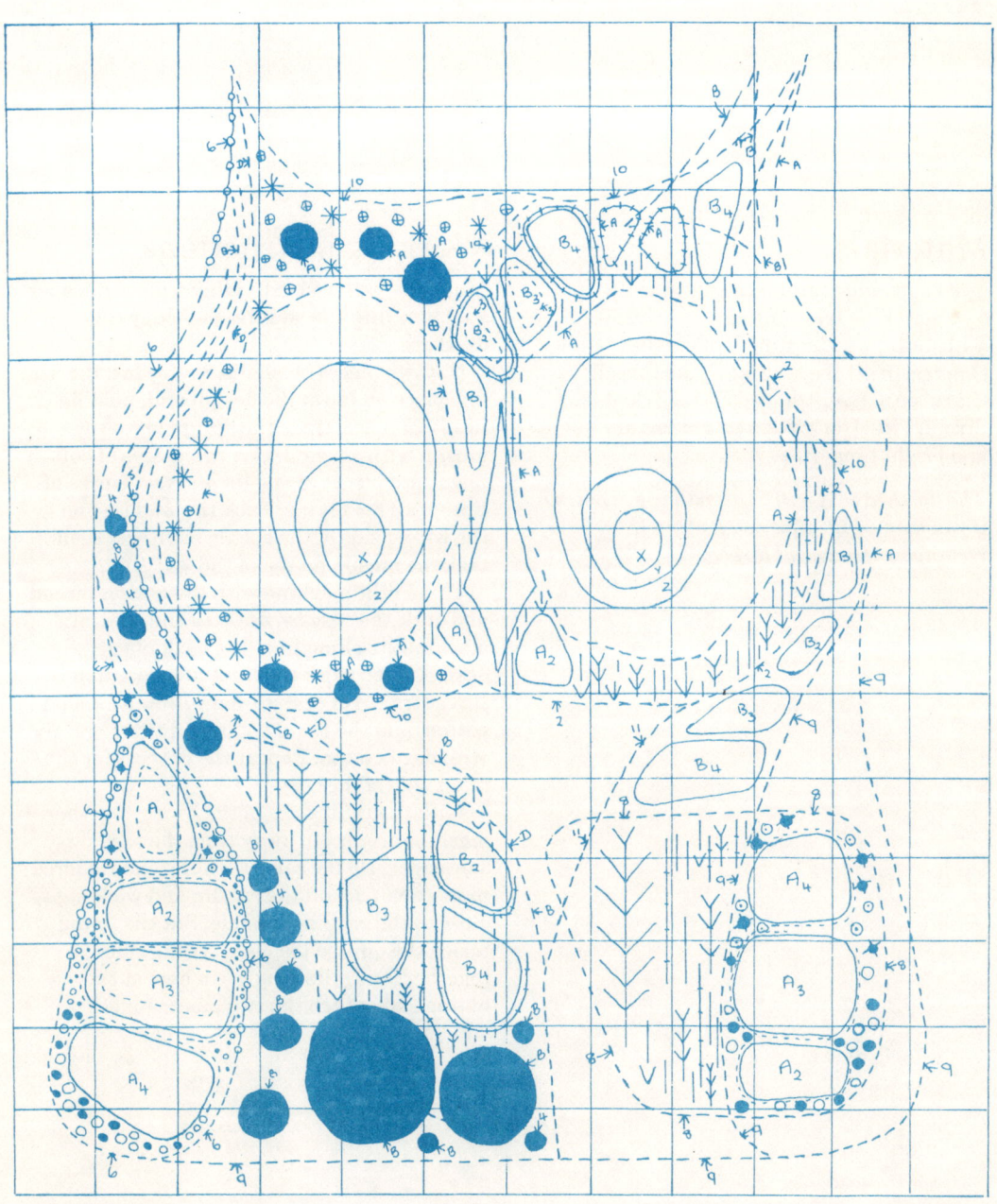

Embroidery for bazaars

Quilted coffee cosy

Materials

$\frac{1}{2}$ yd 36 ins wide turquoise cotton lawn
$\frac{1}{2}$ yd matching tricel lining
$\frac{1}{2}$ yd cotton wadding and $\frac{1}{2}$ yd muslin
One reel [ball] of matching Sylko thread
Clark's Anchor Stranded cotton [Coats Six Strand Floss], one skein bright canary yellow and bright tangerine

The finished cosy will fit a small coffee pot, so if you have a big coffee pot, just cut the rectangles of material larger

Working instructions

Make the pattern by dividing a piece of paper 8 × 14 ins into 1 in squares and copy the diagram.

Cut two pieces of muslin 8 × 13$\frac{1}{2}$ ins. Place one piece on top of the design and, holding it firmly in place, trace the design on to the muslin with a pencil. Cut two pieces of cotton lawn, two pieces of muslin and two pieces of lining, all 8 × 13$\frac{1}{2}$ ins. Tack the wadding on to the wrong side of the cotton lawn and then tack the muslin on top of the wadding.

Thread the machine with the cotton thread and quilt the cosy by working the rows of machine stitching from the back of the design. Then work the lines of backstitch in three strands of orange and yellow stranded cotton, and the French knots in three and six strands of cotton. Repeat the process for the other side of the cosy.

With the right sides of the lining together, machine stitch $\frac{1}{2}$ in away from the top and side edges. Do the same with the embroidered pieces and trim off the muslin and wadding as close to the edge as possible. Put the lining inside the quilted tea cosy, wrong sides together, and, allowing a $\frac{1}{2}$ in hem at the bottom, slip stitch the two pieces together.

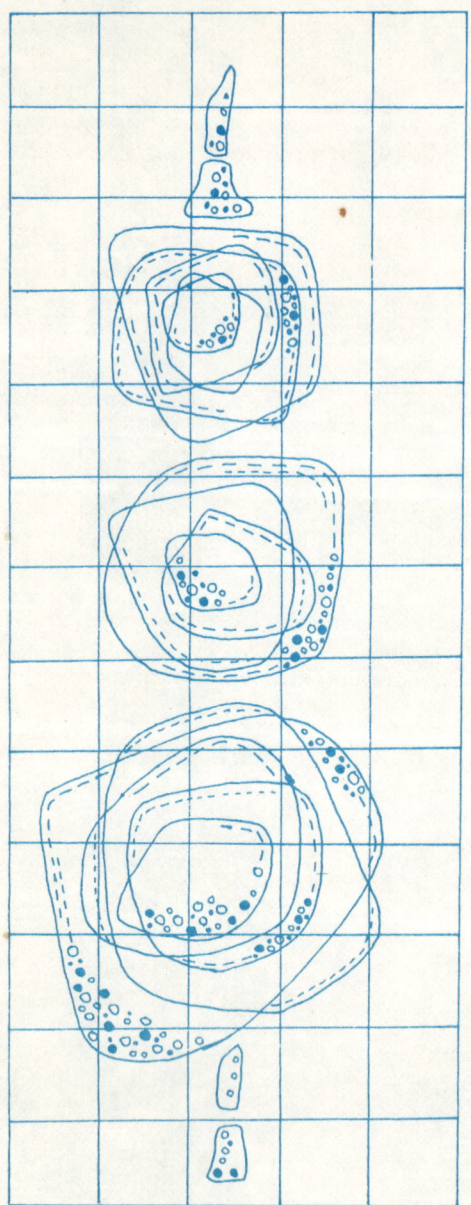

○ *bright canary yellow, large French knots*
○ *bright canary yellow, small French knots*
● *bright tangerine, large French knots*
• *bright tangerine, small French knots*
-----*bright canary yellow, backstitch*
---*bright tangerine, backstitch*

Florentine spectacle case

Materials

$\frac{1}{4}$ yd single thread tapestry canvas 18 ins wide, 18 threads to 1 in
Anchor Tapisserie wool [tapestry yarn], two skeins each of nos. 556,0107 and one skein each of nos. 557,803 and 805.
Two pieces of tricel lining $2\frac{3}{4} \times 7\frac{1}{4}$ ins

for colour illustration, see page 61

Working instructions

Cut two pieces of canvas 9 × 4 ins and mark the centre of the canvas both ways with a line of basting stitches. The arrows on the design indicate the centre of the design which should coincide with the intersection of the basting stitches.

Start to embroider at the centre of the design and, working over four threads of the canvas and following the colour guide, work the first quarter of the design indicated by the broken line. Work the other quarters to match. Then with the purple wool [yarn], work the border round the outside, working the horizontal stitches last of all.

Work the purple border on the other piece of canvas exactly as for the front and fill in the rest of the canvas with rows of vertical stitches over four threads of canvas in colour no.556.

To make up, trim the canvas to within $\frac{1}{2}$ in of the embroidery on all sides. With the right sides of the embroidery together, backstitch the two pieces together as close as possible to the edge of the embroidery, leaving a $1\frac{1}{2}$ in gap at either side at the top of the case (not including the seam allowance at the top).

With the right sides together, machine stitch the two pieces of lining together taking in a $\frac{3}{4}$ in seam and leaving the same sized gap in the top as for the case. Turn the case to the right side and insert the lining into the case. Turn in the seam allowance along the top and side edges and slipstitch the lining to the case.

Cut six 17 ins lengths of purple wool [yarn], plait [braid] them and slipstitch the plait [braid] round the edge of the case.

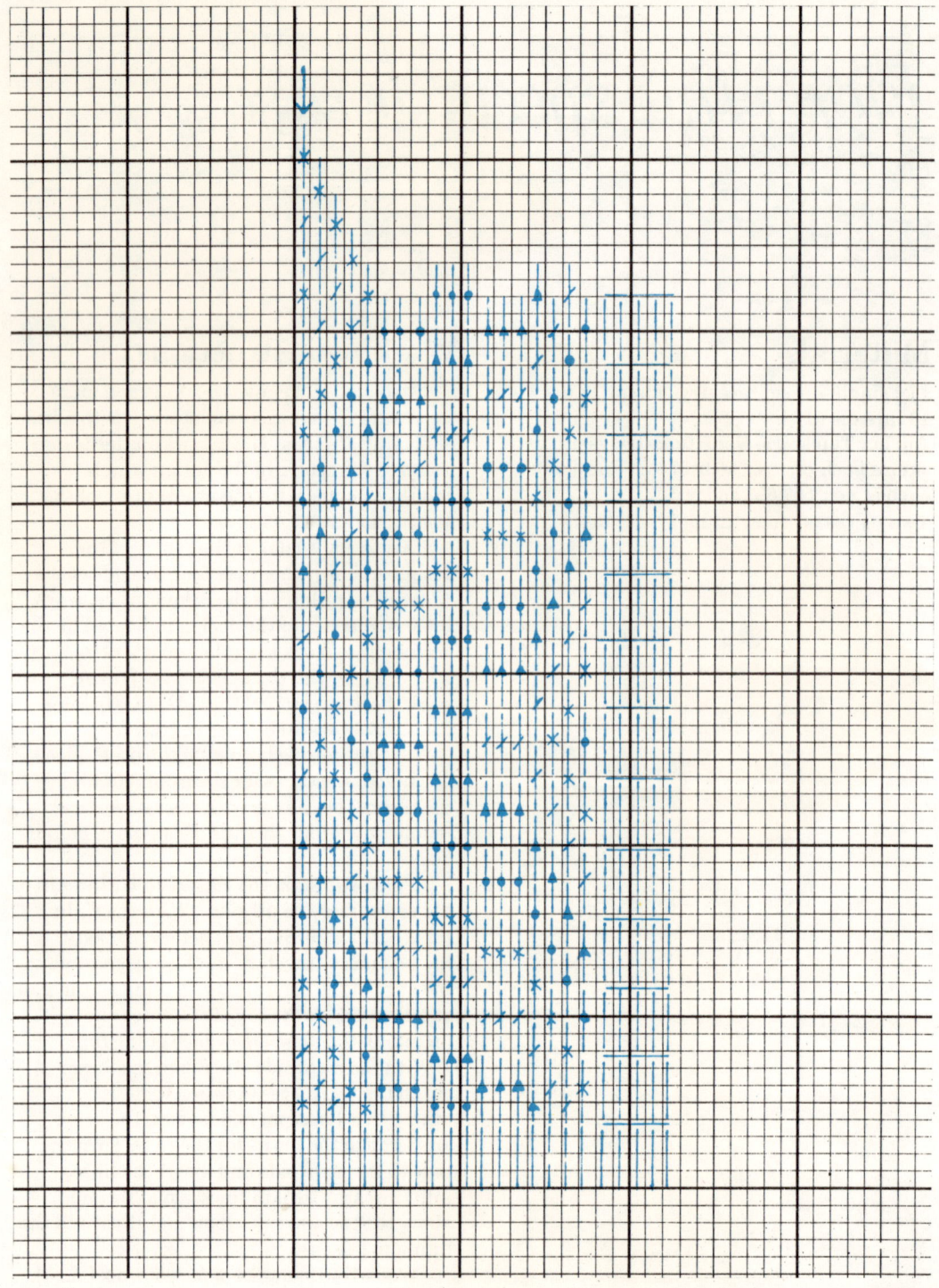

* 556
▲ 557
⁄ 803
● 805
| 0107

Canvas work greeting card

for colour illustration, see page 65

Sampler, embroidered with coloured silks and linen thread in satin, cross, rococo, back stitches and French knots on linen with insertions of Hollie point. Mid 18th Century

Materials

Small quantities of different coloured tapestry wool [yarn]

Working instructions

The card is a sampler of canvas [needlepoint] stitches, so the beginner will find it easy to make something pleasing and useful at the same time. There is no diagram, because you may well want to make up your own sampler, using different variations of these stitches.

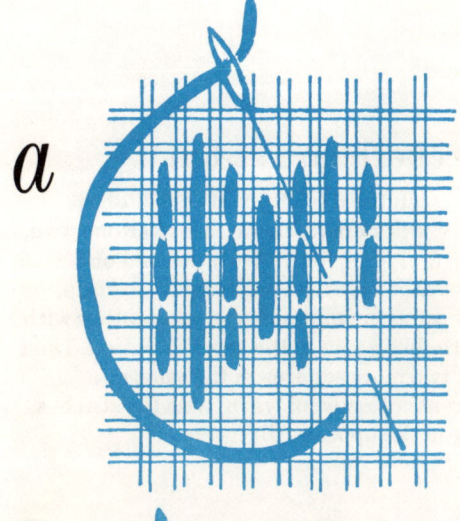

a

Hungarian stitch

Work upright stitches from left to right over two, four and two double threads of canvas. Miss a hole and repeat these three stitches until you reach the end of the line. Work a second line in the same or a different coloured wool [yarn], between the spaces in the previous row.

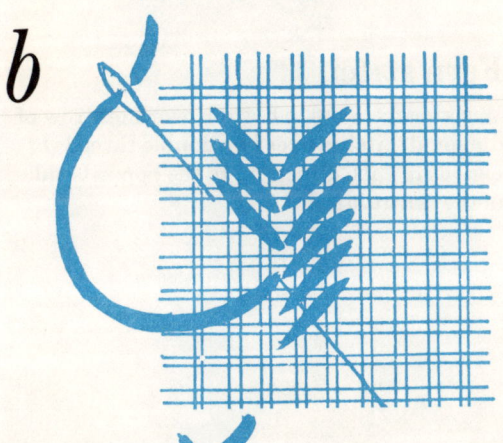

b

Stem stitch

Work a row of diagonal stitches from top to bottom over two double threads of canvas, in each direction. Complete the stitch by working another row in the opposite direction and then working a row of backstitch down the centre of the rows in a different colour.

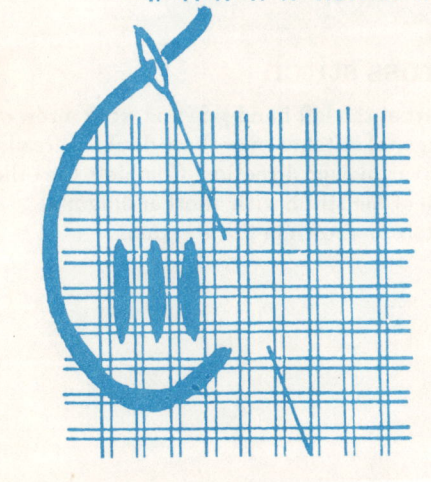

c

Upright gobelin stitch

Working from left to right and bottom to top, work upright stitches over three double threads of canvas in each direction, next to one another.

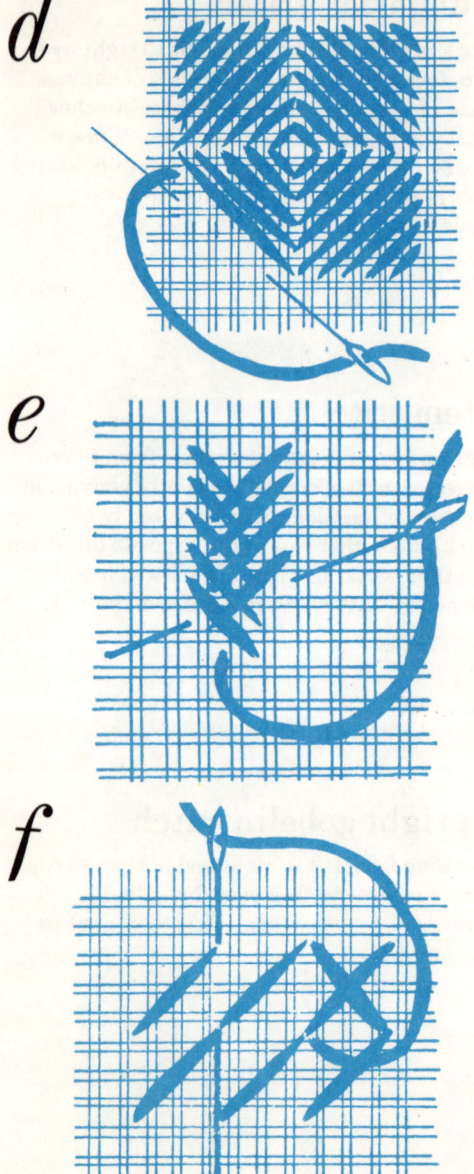

d

Checkerboard stitch

Starting in the top left hand corner of the
square, work diagonal stitches over one, two,
three, four, five, four, three, two and one
double threads of canvas to form a square.
Work another square in the same colour with
the stitches going in the same direction. Then
work two more squares in the same or a
different colour wool [yarn] with the stitches
going in the opposite direction.

e

Fern stitch

Working from top to bottom, work one row of
diagonal stitches over two double threads of
canvas in each direction, to the opposite side
of the centre stitch.

f

Cross stitch

Start at the left hand side and work a row of
diagonal stitches over three double threads of
canvas in each direction. Complete the other
half of the stitch with another diagonal
stitch, as shown in the diagram.

g

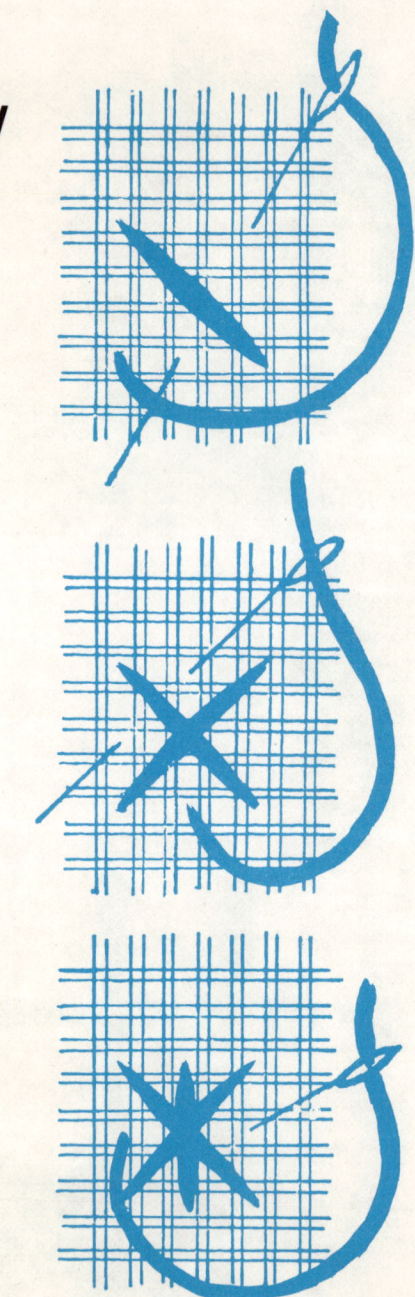

Double cross stitch

Work a single cross stitch over four double threads of canvas in each direction and complete the second stitch as shown in the diagram.

h

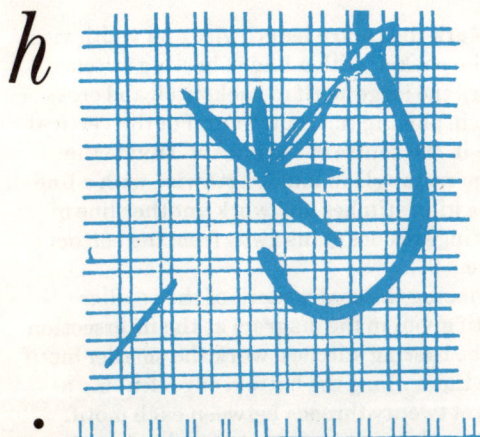

Star stitch

This stitch consists of eight stitches all meeting in the centre hole. Work over two double threads of canvas in each direction until all eight stitches are completed.

i

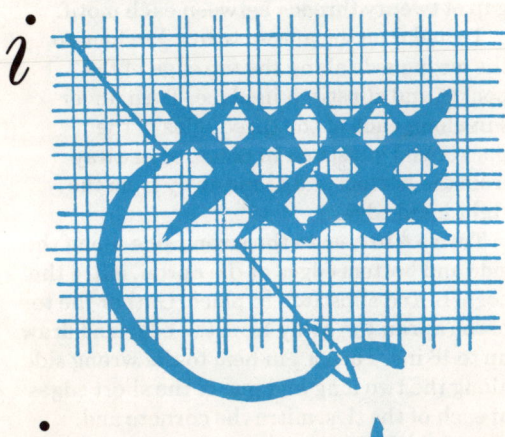

Rice stitch

Work a row of ordinary cross stitch over four double threads of canvas in each direction. Then, using a thinner wool [yarn] in a different colour if possible, work diagonal stitches over the arms of the crosses, meeting in the space between the crosses.

j

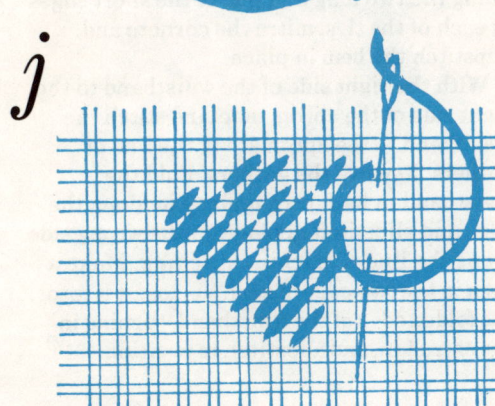

Mosaic stitch

Work diagonal stitches over one and two double threads of canvas alternately until the row is completed; then work another row, working a small stitch into a large one and vice versa.

Blackwork apron

Materials

$\frac{3}{4}$ yd 54 ins wide turquoise evenweave linen,
25 threads to 1 in
One reel [ball] of matching Sylko thread
Clark's Anchor Stranded cotton [Coats Six
Strand Floss], three skeins of black

Working instructions

From the linen, cut a piece $30\frac{1}{2} \times 16\frac{1}{2}$ ins for
the apron, a piece $8 \times 7\frac{1}{2}$ ins for the pocket,
two pieces $24\frac{1}{2} \times 4$ ins for the ties and a piece
4×17 ins for the waistband.

Mark the centre lengthwise and widthwise
of the pocket, with a line of basting stitches.
Work the large motif in backstitch and cross
stitch, placing the centre motif of the vertical
line in the centre of the pocket. Divide the
large rectangle in half lengthwise with a line
of basting stitches and work another line of
basting stitches $4\frac{1}{4}$ ins away from the bottom
edge.

Placing the centre motif of the smaller
motif given in the diagram at the intersection
of the basting stitches, work the smaller motif
five times along the bottom edge, leaving a
gap of twenty threads between each motif.

To make up the apron, turn a $\frac{1}{2}$ in hem to
the wrong side along the top edge of the
pocket and slipstitch in place. Turn under
$\frac{1}{2}$ in along each of the three sides of the
pocket and slipstitch in place, $5\frac{3}{4}$ in away
from the bottom and $4\frac{1}{2}$ ins away from the
right hand edge.

Turn a $\frac{1}{2}$ in hem to the wrong side along the
side and bottom edges of the apron, mitre the
corners and slipstitch in place. Gather the top
of the apron $\frac{1}{2}$ in away from the edge and draw
up to 16 ins. Turn a $\frac{1}{2}$ in hem to the wrong side
along the two long and one of the short edges
of each of the ties, mitre the corners and
slipstitch the hem in place.

With the right side of the waistband to the
right side of the apron, machine stitch the
waistband to the apron along the line of
gathers. Remove the gathers. Fold the
waistband in half, turn under $\frac{1}{2}$ in along the
edge and slipstitch in place on the wrong side,
along the line of machine stitching. Make a
tuck in the raw edge of each tie, insert it into
the folded edge of the waistband, turning in
the extra $\frac{1}{2}$ in, and slipstitch in position.

for detail, see page 17

Needlecase and pincushion

Materials

$\frac{1}{4}$ yd 36 ins wide red evenweave linen
Two pieces of red Binca canvas 4 ins square.
for the inside of the needlecase
Scraps of black, blue and green felt
Clark's Anchor Stranded cotton [Coats Six Strand Floss], one skein of lemon yellow and one skein of white
Sylko Perle cotton [perle cotton], no.5 thickness, one ball each of nos.769,774,758 and navy blue.

Working instructions

Cut four pieces of red fabric $6\frac{1}{2}$ ins square. Trace the design on to tracing paper and transfer it on to the right side of the fabric on two of the squares, but putting carbon paper face down on the fabric underneath the tracing paper and drawing over the lines of the design with a pencil. Using the tracing as a pattern, cut three pieces of black felt for the body, two pieces of green and two pieces of blue for the wings and oversew [overcast] them in position.

Work the lines of yellow knot stitch in six strands of stranded cotton. Then work the lines of backstitch in yellow, blue and red Sylko Perle [perle cotton], and the French knots in navy blue Sylko Perle [perle cotton] and six strands of stranded cotton.

Complete the other butterfly in the same way.

To make up the pincushion, thread the machine with red cotton, put one of the plain squares next to one of the embroidered squares, wrong sides together, and machine stitch round three sides of the square, $\frac{1}{2}$ in away from the edge. Stuff firmly with kapok and machine stitch the last side together. Fray the material around the edges as far as the machine stitching.

To finish the needlecase, stitch one plain and one embroidered square together along the left hand side, $\frac{1}{2}$ in away from the edge. Then machine stitch the two pieces of Binca to the inside of the plain piece of fabric, $\frac{1}{2}$ in away from the machine stitched outer edge. Fray the edge of the fabric that is machine stitched and fray $\frac{1}{2}$ in on the other three sides.

for colour illustration, see page 73

O *Navy blue French knots, Sylko Perle*   ∞ *white chain stitch, stranded cotton*
• *White French knots, stranded cotton*   ···· *white backstitch, stranded cotton*
+++*lemon yellow, knot stitch*   ·|·|·| *774*
---*758, backstitch*   •-• *769*
                                           --- *758*

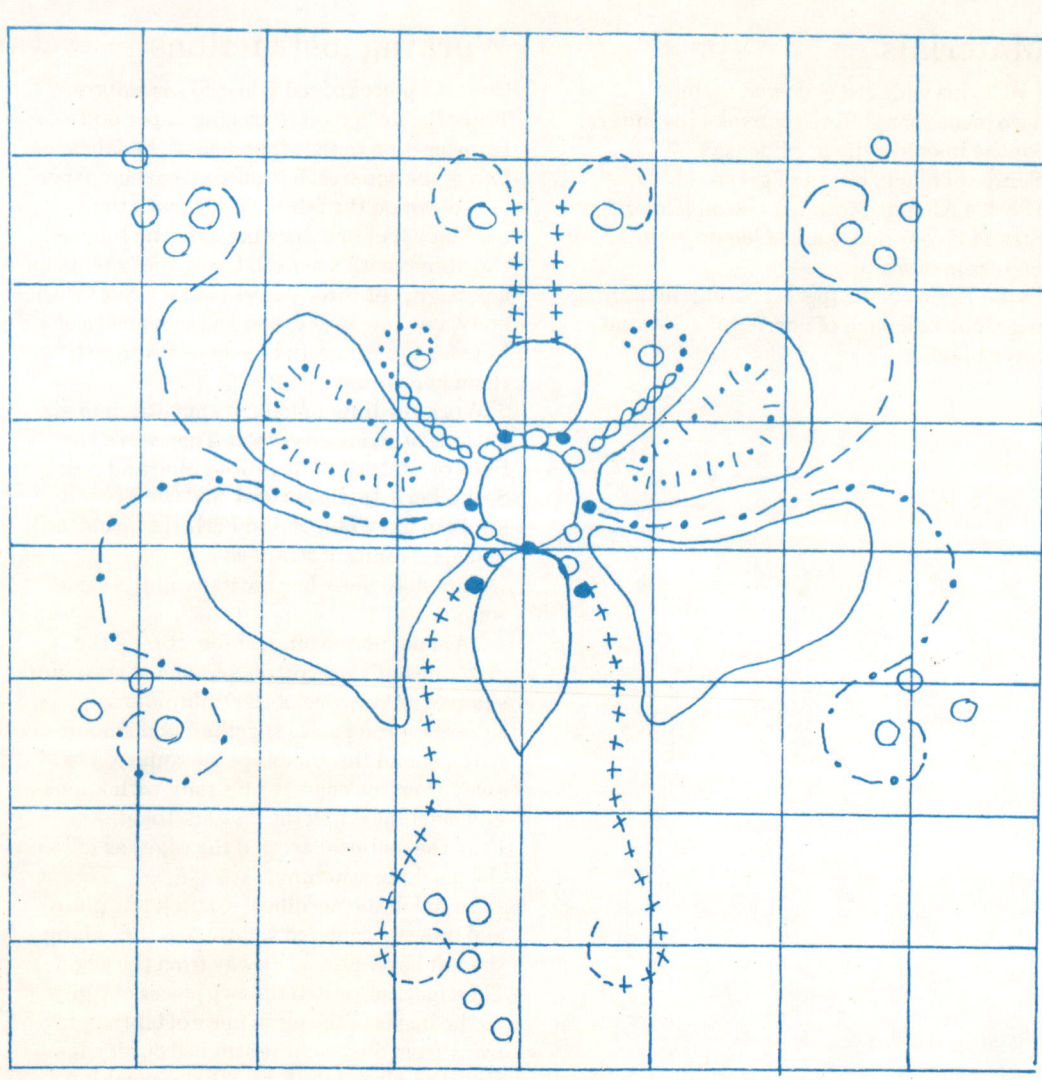

Dress embroidery

Evening bag

Materials

½ yd 36 ins wide evenweave yellow furnishing [upholstery] fabric
A piece of pale lemon silk Duppion fabric 15 × 9 ins
A piece of cotton wadding, 6 × 11 ins
Scraps of yellow and white felt
Small pieces of gold and lemon kid
¼ yd gold and iridescent braid, 1½ in wide
One reel [ball] of gold thread
One ball of pale lemon chenille wool [yarn]
One reel [ball] of pale lemon thread
One ball of Sylko Perle cotton [perle cotton], thickness no.8, no.839
Clark's Anchor Stranded cotton [Coats Six Strand Floss], one skein of white
Four rectangular lemon plastic shapes with holes in them (if you cannot find any, use acetate as a substitute)
Twenty-two ¼ in brass studs
Eighteen barrel-shaped gold beads
Three square gold painted wooden beads
Twelve medium and twenty-five small round gold-painted wooden beads
Twenty-five bright yellow beads
One hundred small white chalk beads and eighty small gold beads
Ten semi-circular white beads and eight medium and small-sized white beads
Three gold tambour beads

✺ large gold wooden bead and gold stitches
✳ small gold wooden bead and gold stitches
◎ large gold wooden bead with tambour bead on top
✿ semi-circular white beads with white stitches through the centre
O medium sized white bead
⚥ small white bead with stitches through the centre
⊕ bead covered with gold kid
✸ square gold wooden bead with gold stitches
⬬ small gold beads
⬭ white chalk beads
• small yellow beads
/// iridescent braid
✚ plastic shape and stitches
1 gold kid
2 lemon leather over the top of a brass stud
3 gold kid over the top of a brass stud
4 lemon kid
5 padded lemon kid
6 yellow felt
7 white felt

Both section As are single satin stitch in gold thread and lime green chenille wool.
Section C is single satin stitch in gold thread and gold barrel beads.

for colour illustration, see page 77

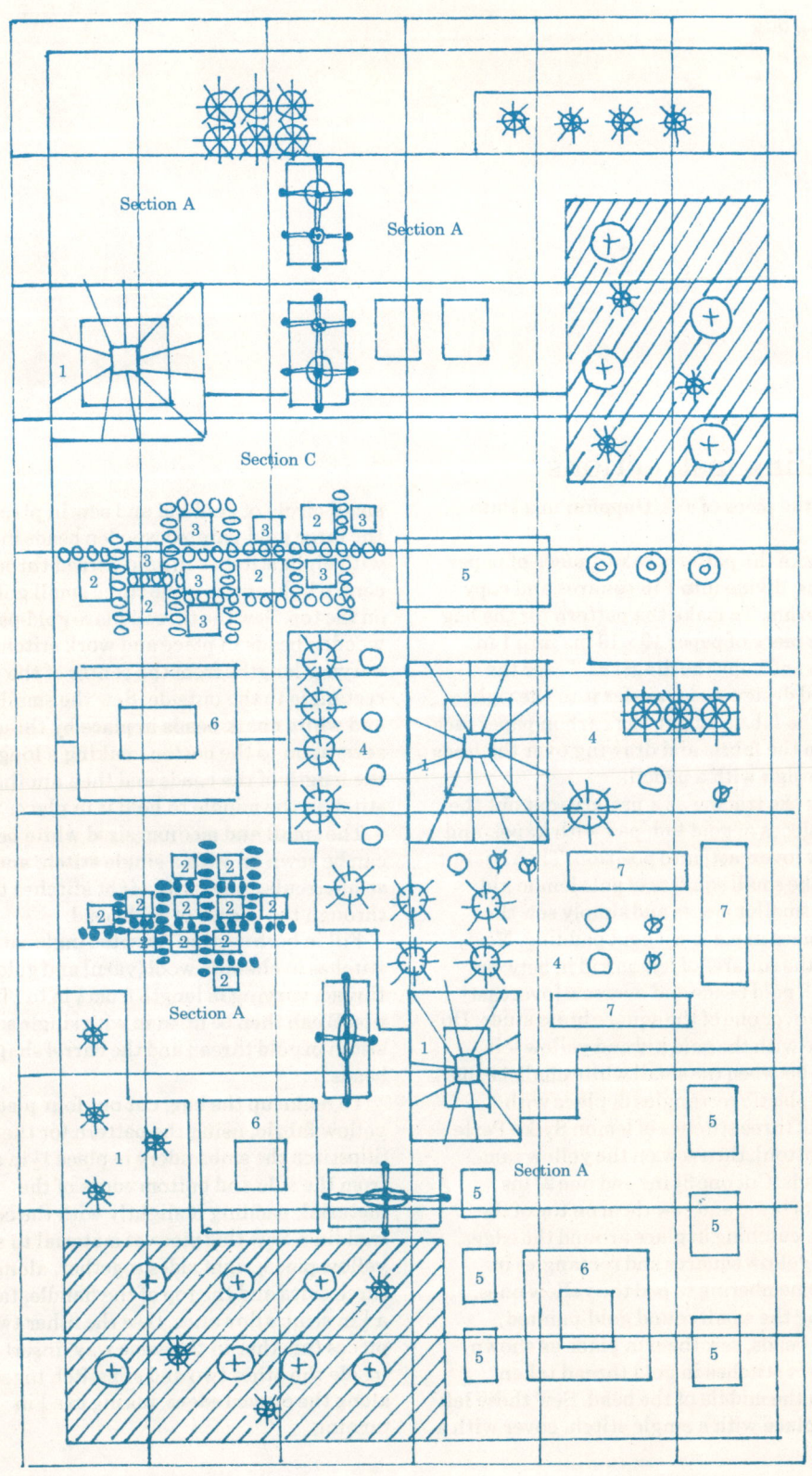

Working instructions

Mount the piece of silk Duppion in a slate frame.

To make the pattern, take a piece of paper 12 × 6 ins, divide into 1 in squares and copy the diagram. To make the pattern for the bag, divide a piece of paper 10 × 19 ins into 1 in squares and copy the diagram. Trace the enlarged design and transfer it to the right side of the fabric by putting carbon paper face down on the fabric and drawing over the lines of the design with a pencil.

Using the tracing as a pattern, cut out the larger pieces of gold kid, pad with kapok and oversew [overcast] into position. Then cut out all but the small squares of pale lemon kid, pad the smaller pieces and simply sew the larger piece in place without padding. Next, cut out the squares of lemon kid in between the small gold beads and oversew [overcast] in place over one of the square brass studs. Do the same with the gold kid and yellow felt squares between the small white chalk beads. Sew the plastic rectangles in place with groups of three stitches of lemon Sylko Perle [perle cotton], then sew on the yellow tambour beads. Cut one $3\frac{1}{2}$ ins and one $2\frac{1}{2}$ ins lengths of braid and sew them on top of the gold kid, catching in place around the edges. Sew the yellow squares and rectangles in place, remembering to pad the yellow ones.

Taking the small round gold-painted wooden beads, sew them in place as shown, with eight stitches in gold thread taken through the middle of the bead. Sew those left over in place with a single stitch, cover with a small circle of gold kid and sew in place. Sew the large gold-painted wooden beads in place with eight stitches in gold thread through the centre hole and sew the three small gold beads on the top. Sew the three square gold-painted wooden beads in place and work stitches in varying lengths from the centre of the rectangle to the outside. Sew the small gold and white chalk beads in place by threading several on to the cotton, making a long stitch the length of the beads and then another stitch in the middle to hold it in place.

The small and medium sized white beads can be sewn on with a single stitch, and the semi-circular ones with eight stitches taken through the centre of each bead.

Fill in both section As with single satin stitches in chenille wool [yarn] and gold thread, varying in length from $\frac{1}{8}$ in to 1 in. Section B can then be filled in with single satin stitch in gold thread and the barrel shaped beads.

To make up the bag, cut out four pieces in yellow fabric, using the pattern for the bag. Slipstitch the embroidery in place $1\frac{1}{2}$ in away from the side and bottom edges of the material, padding it slightly with the cotton wadding. Sew this piece of material to another yellow piece, right sides together, along the three sides and the top of the handle, taking in a $\frac{1}{2}$ in seam allowance. Sew the other two pieces together in the same way, insert them inside the other two and slipstitch together along the curved edges, taking in a $\frac{1}{4}$ in turning.

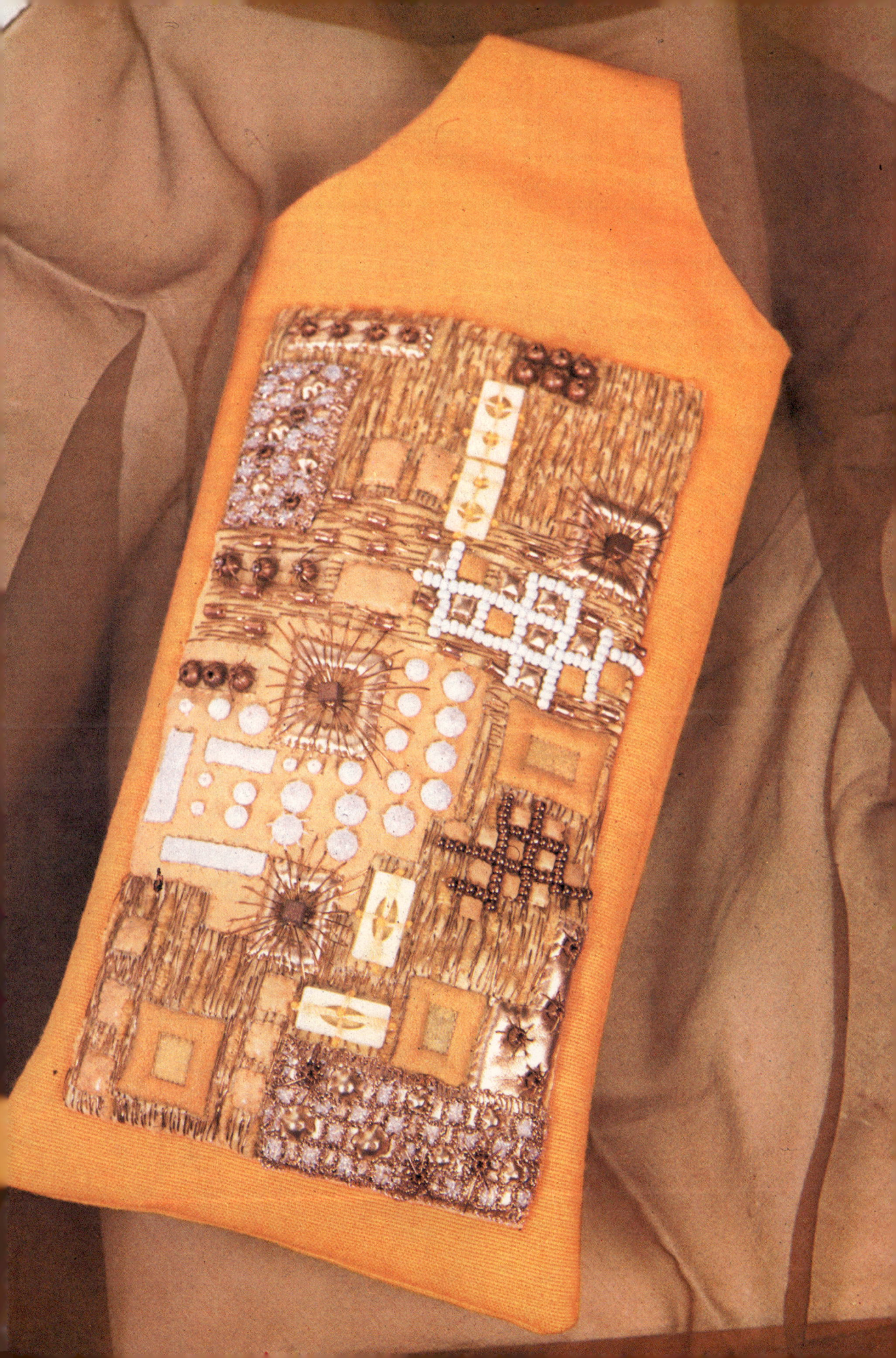

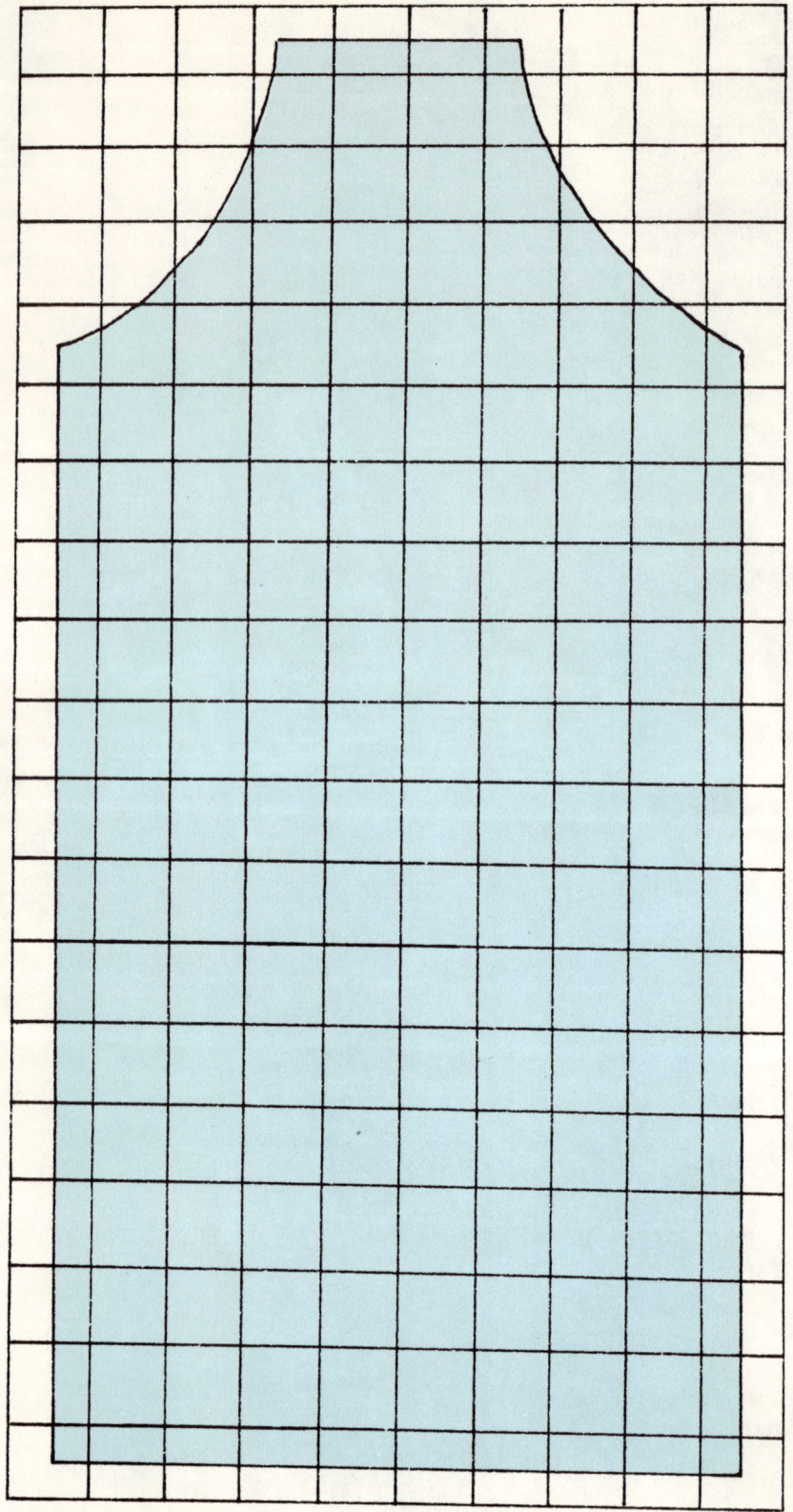

Smock with insertion stitches

Materials

I shall only give the amount needed for the yoke, yoke facings, pockets and sleeve bands, and the pattern for these pieces, because they can be easily used in conjunction with a bought paper pattern similar in style to the smock.

For the yoke, yoke facings, pockets and sleeve bands you need $\frac{3}{4}$ yd 36 ins wide woven cotton material.

One reel [ball] of matching Sylko cotton and Anchor Perle cotton no.5 thickness, one ball of no.0304.

Working instructions

To make the pattern, divide a piece of paper 17×14 ins into 1 in squares and copy the diagram. Trace the yoke and yoke facings and, using the tracing as a pattern, cut out the yoke front and back and facings.

To cut out and embroider the pockets, cut two pieces $8 \times 2\frac{1}{4}$ ins and two pieces $4\frac{1}{4} \times 8$ ins. Taking one of the smaller pieces, turn a single $\frac{1}{4}$ in hem to the wrong side along one of the longer edges and machine stitch in position. Do the same for one of the larger pieces of fabric. Fold over $\frac{1}{2}$ in of fabric to the wrong side along the edge where you have just machine stitched the $\frac{1}{4}$ in turning and tack in place. Do the same for the other pieces.

Tack the two pieces of material on to a thick piece of paper, with the folded edges $\frac{3}{8}$ in apart, and work the buttonhole insertion stitch. When you have completed the stitch, remove the tacking stitches and topstitch $\frac{1}{4}$ in away from the folded edge with the machine.

Turn a $\frac{1}{2}$ in hem to the wrong side along the top of the pocket and machine stitch in place. Turn in $\frac{1}{2}$ in on all the other three sides and tack and machine stitch in place on the garment. Work the other pocket in the same way. Embroider the yoke in the same way as the pocket, hem and sew the facings in place. Turn them to the wrong side and topstitch in place $\frac{1}{4}$ in away from the neck edge.

To make and embroider the sleeve bands, cut two pieces of material 14×4 ins. Fold one of the pieces in half lengthwise and work a row of knotted insertion stitch or Antwerp Edging along the edge. Sew the band to the sleeve edge.

for colour illustration, see page 81

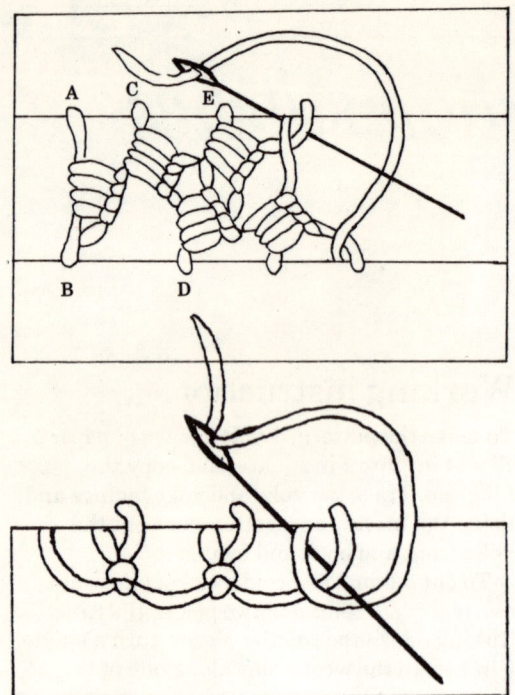

Buttonhole insertion stitch

Tack the two strips of material on to the paper as described in the instructions. Bring the needle through the material at A, insert again at B and bring it out under the edge of the material. Work four buttonhole stitches on the first crossbar of the thread and insert the needle at C, from the upper to the underside of the material, then pull it over the first part of the stitch (see diagram). Make another stitch in this way at D, a little lower than C, and work four buttonhole stitches over the looped stitch at C, working from the centre towards the edge. Make another looped stitch on the right at E, then work four buttonhole stitches on the looped stitch at D. Carry on in this way until you reach the end of the line.

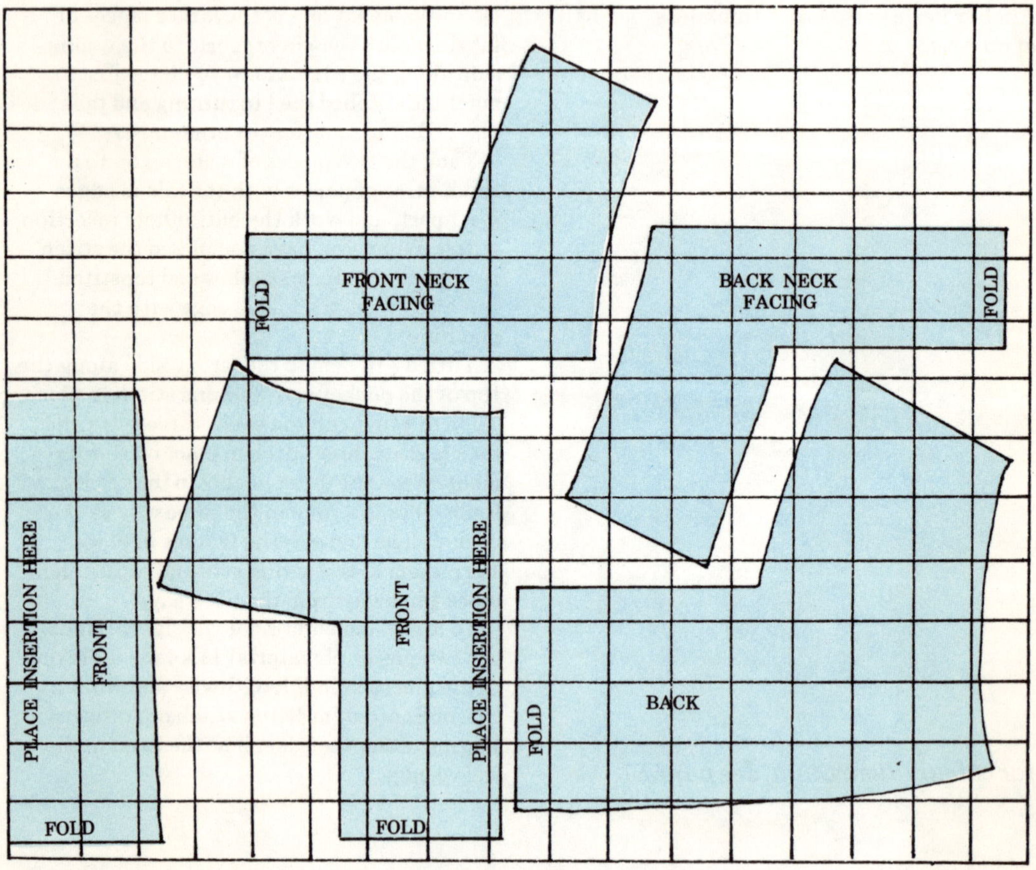

FOLD

FRONT NECK FACING

BACK NECK FACING

FOLD

PLACE INSERTION HERE

FRONT

FRONT

PLACE INSERTION HERE

FOLD

BACK

FOLD

FOLD

Embroidered jacket

Materials

1 yd 48 ins wide material with an exciting design that suggests certain shapes to you, such as the screen printed linen which I found, suggesting a butterfly
1 yd matching lining material
1 yd of terylene or cotton wadding
One reel [ball] of matching Sylko thread
One ball of red and one ball of white Sylko Perle cotton [perle cotton], no.5 thickness
Twenty-three large white beads
Seventy-seven small white beads
Ten large pink wooden beads
Eight large red wooden beads
Eight white plastic dome shapes
Six silver plastic dome shapes
Twenty-six oval silver sequins
Four large white plastic rings and two small ones
One circle of silver acetate
Scraps of silver kid
Thick- and medium-thick silver thread for couching

for colour illustration, see page 85

Working instructions

I shall give you general directions as I did for the hat, because the design on your material will not be the same as on mine.

The main idea is to see how one can develop a design by using the fabric as a guide, instead of drawing and tracing a design.

To make the pattern for the jacket, divide a piece of paper 16 × 32 ins into 1 in squares and copy the diagram. Cut out the fronts and back of the jacket in the jacket material, lining and wadding. Tack the wadding to the wrong side of the jacket front and backs and quilt it along the lines of the design on the fabric.

Mount the front of the jacket in a slate frame and start to embroider. The body is made up of a circle of silver acetate, two silver dome shapes for the head and eight oval silver sequins held in place by straight stitches in red and white Sylko Perle [perle cotton], and small white beads are sewn between the sequins.

The two bottom wings consist of a white plastic ring on top of which are sewn five sequins, held in place by a small white bead. A silver dome shape in the centre is surrounded by five large white beads which have a pink wooden bead between each one, held in place by four stitches in white Sylko Perle [perle cotton], taken through the centre of each bead; a small white bead is sewn on top.

The top two wings are made up of a large narrow white ring and a small thick white ring in the centre of the larger one. Four sequins go over the outer ring and under the inner one, and are held in place by a red wooden bead with three stitches of white Sylko Perle [perle cotton] taken through the centre. Between each sequin on the outer ring is sewn a white dome shape and a small white

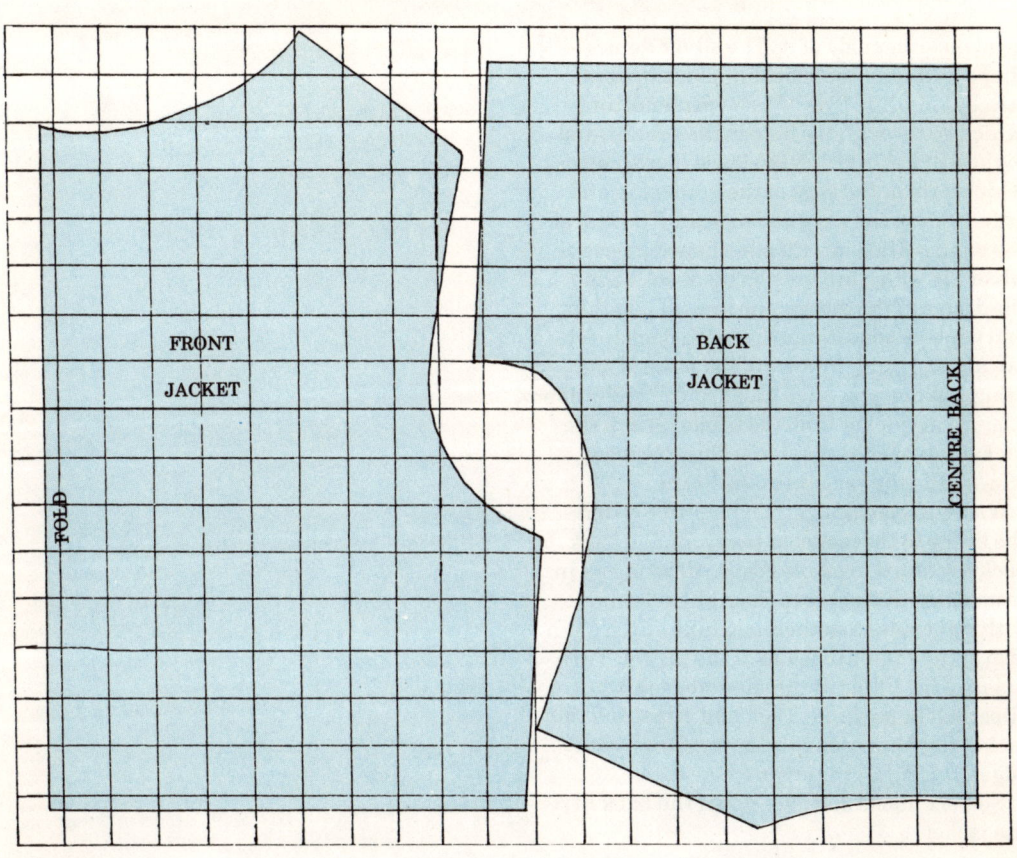

bead on either side of it. The silver dome
shape in the centre is held in place by four
stitches in white Sylko Perle [perle cotton]
which go through the hole in the sequin, and
eight stitches in red Sylko Perle [perle cotton]
which go over the edge of the inner ring and
either side of the red wooden bead. The rest of
the wing is filled in with odd-shaped pieces of
silver kid which are sewn in place following
the design of the fabric. The lines of couching
and white beads alternating with backstitch
are also working following the lines of the
design. When you have finished the embroidery,
remove the jacket from the frame. Stitch the
jacket together at the side seams, taking in
$\frac{1}{2}$ in, and do the same with the lining.

With right sides together, machine stitch
the lining to the jacket at the front and back
neck edges and armhole edges, allowing a $\frac{1}{2}$ in
seam. Turn the jacket to the right side and
with right sides together, machine stitch a $\frac{1}{2}$ in
hem at the shoulder seams of the jacket. Turn
in $\frac{1}{2}$ in of the lining at the shoulders and
slipstitch in position. Tack and slipstitch the
jacket together along the bottom and back
edges, taking a $\frac{1}{2}$ in turning.

Sew six hooks and eyes down the back of
the jacket.

Embroidered belt

Materials

$\frac{1}{4}$ yd 36 ins wide orange evenweave furnishing [upholstery] fabric.
$\frac{1}{4}$ yd orange lining
$\frac{1}{4}$ yd heavyweight interfacing
$\frac{3}{8}$ yd 36 ins muslin
Two yds orange or yellow cord
Matching Sylko cotton
Scraps of medium and bright pink and dark purple felt
One skein of dark purple tapestry wool [yarn]
Sylko Perle cotton [perle cotton], thickness no.5, one ball each of nos.0100,26,830 and no.8 thickness, one ball of no.830
Anchor Stranded cotton [Coats Six Strand Floss], one skein of wine-mauve
Four large purple wooden beads
Two large pink wooden beads
Eight $\frac{1}{2}$ in diameter curtain rings and four 1 in diameter curtain rings

for colour illustration, see page 89

Working instructions

Divide a piece of paper 13 × 8 ins into 1 in squares and copy the diagram of the shape of the belt. Fold the fabric in half widthwise, right sides together; then placing the pattern on the foldline as indicated, cut out the shape in lining, interfacing and orange furnishing [upholstery] fabric.

Mount the piece of muslin in a slate frame and tack the piece of evenweave linen to be embroidered on to the linen, right side facing upwards. From the embroidery diagram, trace the shapes of the pieces of felt and the placement of the curtain rings. With the tracing placed centrally on the left front of the belt, $1\frac{1}{2}$ ins away from all the edges, tack along the lines you have traced and pull the tracing paper away. Trace the same lines again, reverse the tracing and transfer the design to the other side.

Cut out the felt shapes in the colours indicated. Pad them with kapok and oversew [overcast] in position. Cover one large curtain ring with dark purple stranded cotton in buttonhole stitch and one with purple Sylko Perle cotton [perle cotton]. Slipstitch in position. Cover two of the smaller rings with purple stranded cotton, one in dark purple stranded cotton and one in pink Sylko Perle [perle cotton]; slipstitch in place. Work the Spiders' Webs in the three outer rings and sew the beads in the three small rings with eight stitches taken through the centres, following the colour guide. Work the French knots in dark purple wool [yarn] and bright pink Sylko Perle cotton [perle cotton].

Repeat this for the other side.

To make up the belt, remove the work from the frame and cut the muslin away as close to the wrong side of the fabric as possible. Tack the interfacing to the wrong side of the lining. Cut the cord into four 18 ins lengths and knot each piece at one end. Sew the un-knotted ends to the right side of the fabric with the frayed end facing the raw edge of the fabric. With the right side of the embroidery to the right side of the lining and interfacing and making sure that the cord is inside the belt, tack and machine stitch the belt together taking a $\frac{1}{2}$ in seam and leaving a gap between c and d.

Turn the belt to the right side, slipstitch C and D and press with a damp cloth and hot iron.

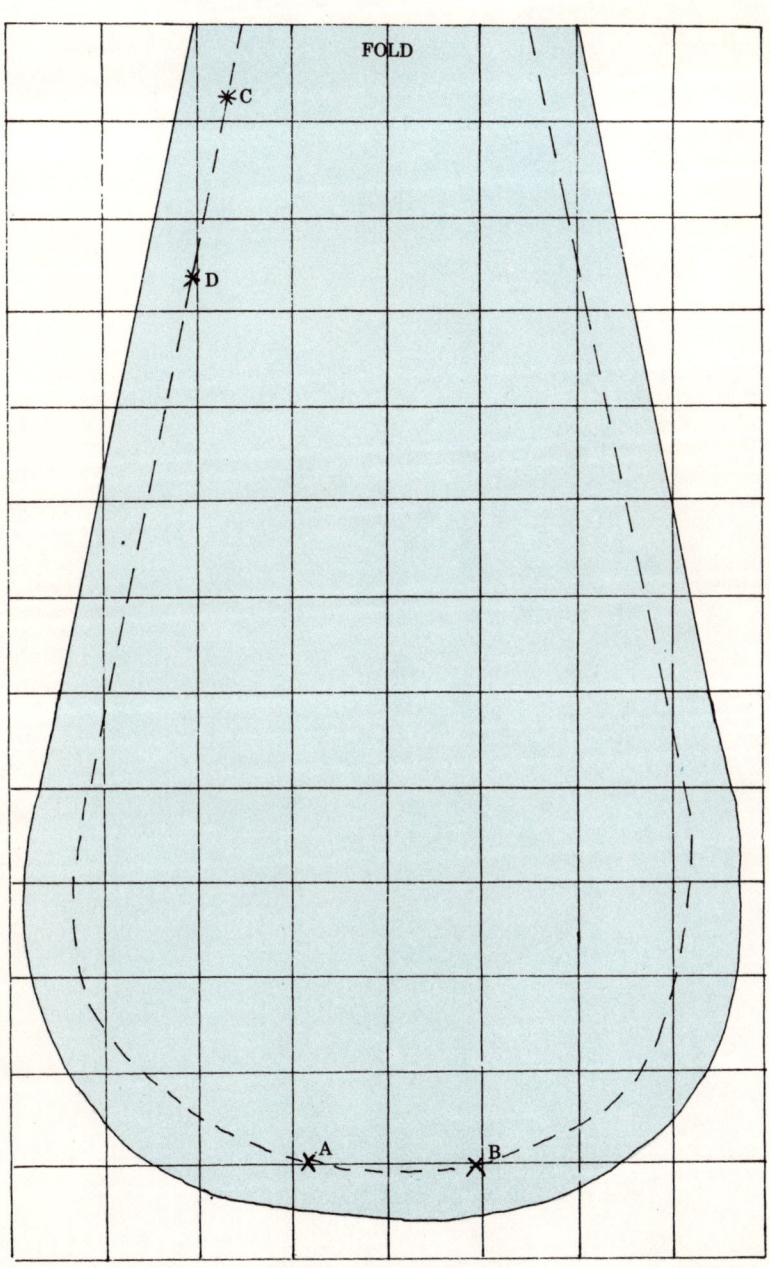

Embroidered belt

● dark purple wool French knots
○ 26, Sylko Perle French knots
C wine-mauve, Spider's web
D wine-mauve, Spider's web
E 0100, Spider's web
F wine-mauve, ring covered
G 0100, ring covered
H 830, ring covered

1 bright pink felt
2 medium pink felt
3 dark purple felt
A dark purple wooden beads
B pink wooden beads

*All the foundation stitches of the Spider's web
are worked in Sylko Perle no.830.*

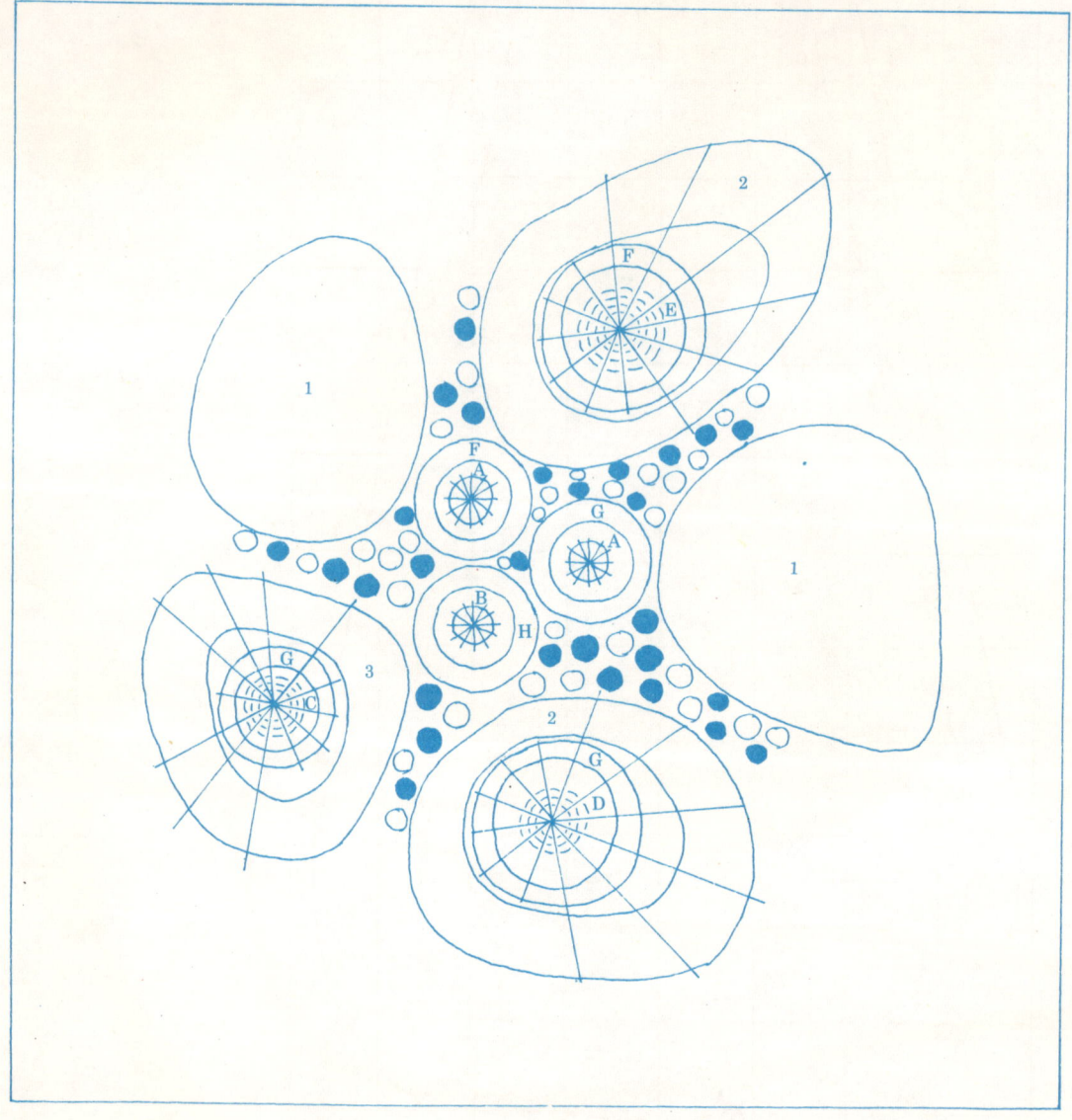

Embroidered pocket

Materials

A piece of blue evenweave linen, 8 × 10 ins
Scraps of blue, green and silver leather
Nine small green wooden beads
Seven plastic silver dome shapes
$\frac{1}{2}$ yd thick silver thread
1 yd medium thick silver thread
Sylko Perle cotton [perle cotton], thickness no.5, one ball each of nos.0257 and 0188 and one ball of nos.769 and 924, no.8 thickness
Matching Sylko thread in white, green and blue.

Working instructions

Trace the outlines of the pieces of leather, silver dome shapes and lines of medium thick silver thread, from the diagram. Transfer this design to the fabric by placing a piece of carbon face down on the right side of the material, underneath the design, and drawing over the lines of the design with a pencil.

Mount the fabric in a slate frame.

Work the embroidery by closely following the diagram. Pad and sew the leather in place. Cut the centres out of four of the silver dome shapes and sew them and the other shapes in position. Couch the silver thread and sew the green wooden beads in place with three stitches in Sylko Perle cotton [perle cotton], taken through the centre. Work the French knots and, following the diagram, work the lines of backstitch and single satin stitch.

Remove the embroidery from the frame and trim the fabric to within $1\frac{1}{2}$ in of each of the side edges, 1 in of the bottom edge and $1\frac{1}{2}$ in of the top edge of the embroidery. Turn a $\frac{1}{2}$ in hem at the top of the pocket and slipstitch in place. Turn a $\frac{1}{4}$ in turning to the wrong side along the bottom and side edges and tack and slipstitch in place on the garment.

for colour illustration, see page 92

A	*silver kid*
B	*dark green kid*
C	*blue kid*
D	*medium green kid*
+++	*couched silver thread*
o	*silver domes*
⊚	*silver domes with the centres removed*

•	*0257, French knots*
o	*0188, French knots*
–o–	*924, single satin stitch*
–•–	*769, single satin stitch*
–·–·–	*0257, backstitch*
– – – –	*0188, backstitch*

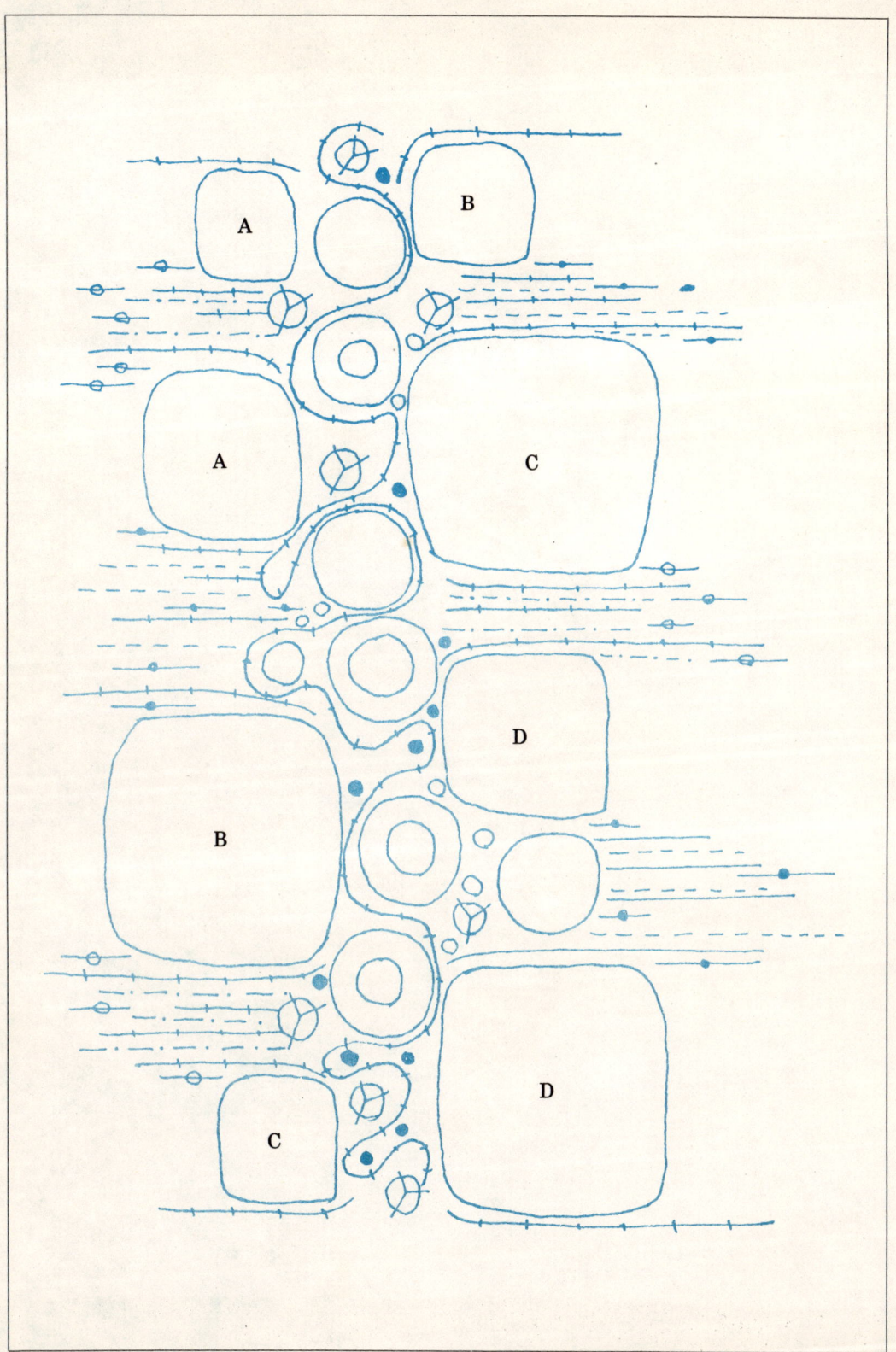